$6.95
Spiral binding
$8.95
USA

Clothes Sense

by Barbara Weiland and Leslie Wood

D0595483

STRAIGHT TALK ABOUT WARDROBE PLANNING

Designed by Linda Wisner
Illustrated by Kate Seigal and Maggie Raguse

We would like to give special thanks to our friends and business associates who shared with us their personal tips on wardrobing for home, business and travel:

Marta Alto
Gail Brown
Cleo Cummings
Karen Dillon
Judy Lindahl
Pati Palmer
Susan Pletsch
Lynn Raasch
Roslyn Simon
Marilyn Thelen

And, a very special thanks to our publishers who were able to turn our mile-high manuscript into a concise and perfectly straightforward book.

Copyright © 1984 Palmer/Pletsch Associates, Ninth printing, 1988.
Library of Congress Catalog Card No. 83-83122
Published by Palmer/Pletsch Associates, P.O. Box 12046
Portland, Oregon, U.S.A. 97212-0046

Design and Production by Wisner Associates, Portland, Oregon
Illustrations by Wisner Associates
Printed by the Irwin-Hodson company, Portland, Oregon, U.S.A.

ISBN 0-935278-10-9

TABLE OF CONTENTS

ABOUT THE AUTHORS...

Barbara Weiland   Leslie Wood

While fashion itself is an art, the art of understanding fashion is something that can easily be learned. Barbara Weiland and Leslie Wood are well-versed in both fashion and teaching. They have put their personal experiences, research and testing together to produce the tools to teach everyone "clothes sense".

Barbara Weiland is a certified color consultant with her own business in Portland, Maine. She is a graduate of Colorado State University with a B.S. in Textiles and Clothing. She has worked for Butterick Fashion Marketing Company, first as a traveling educational representative and later as an editor with Butterick Publishing. Barbara has also been an instructor in Fashion Merchandising at Westbrook College in Maine.

Leslie Wood has her own communications business located in San Francisco, California. While specializing in consumer promotions, she is also involved in seminar planning and management and acts as a media spokesperson for various companies. Leslie graduated with a B.S. degree in Fashion Merchandising from Florida State University. She has worked in fashion retailing in Washington, D.C. and as a fashion stylist for Simplicity Pattern Company in New York. Leslie is currently seen as hostess of the PBS telecourse, "Sewing Power" and appears regularly on "AM San Francisco".

Both Leslie and Barbara are nationally-known sewing and fashion experts and guest lecturers with Palmer/Pletsch Associates, traveling throughout North America giving seminars on sewing and wardrobe planning.

Everyone Needs "Clothes Sense"

We all spend a lot of time, money, and energy getting dressed. It should be a pleasant experience, not a chore. When your closet door opens up to a well-planned wardrobe of coordinated pieces, you spend less time thinking about what to wear and more time enjoying the pieces you own. This is a winning wardrobe and it can be yours. All it takes is a little "clothes sense" — an awareness of fashion, your needs, and your best looks.

As sewing professionals, we believe the best wardrobes are a combination of things you sew and things you buy. However, we wrote **Clothes Sense** for everyone, whether you sew a lot, a little, or not at all. When you buy, the major styling decisions have been made by the designer. When you sew, you are the designer, coordinating patterns and fabric. In both cases, you must evaluate whether an item:

- enhances your figure
- works with what's in your closet
- fits into your budget

We are giving you the tools that will help you understand fashion and make it work **for** you, not against you. You'll learn how to develop a practical wardrobe sewing/buying plan and adjust that plan as your needs change.

Your newly developed "clothes sense" will:

- put an end to tiresome and frustrating wardrobe shopping
- help you feel comfortable, confident, and attractive in the clothes you wear
- take the worry out of what to wear
- make getting dressed an adventure instead of a chore

So, read on to discover how easy and fun it will be to create a closet full of clothes and **always** have something to wear!

Develop Fashion Fluency

To win at wardrobe planning, you must learn to adapt what's in fashion to your personal needs. This means selecting from classics, current fashion trends, and fads.

Fashion — the styles of dress accepted by the general public. The direction in which fashion moves or evolves is called a **fashion trend**, which can be plotted on the following curve:

PEAK

RISE

INTRODUCTION

FALL

The Anatomy of a Fashion Curve

Introduction — A fashion trend is usually introduced by a high fashion designer (haute couture) who creates an expensive one-of-a-kind original. The styles are often **too** extreme for the average person. Many laughed at the "midi" length when it was first introduced in the late 1960's, because the mini had reached its peak and **everyone** was wearing it.

A fad can also introduce a fashion trend. For example, a movie or an ethnic group can start a fad that takes off and becomes a trend.

Rise — Haute couture is copied for mass production by high quality manufacturers. The style may be modified in order to lower prices, but the clothes are still expensive and somewhat extreme.

Peak — Additional modifications have been made to lower the price or to make it less extreme for mass acceptance.

Fall — There is so much of the style that everyone who wants it, has it. It goes on sale in stores and sells well at reduced prices. Stores often continue to buy the style, but only at manufacturers' promotional prices. Finally, either the customer is tired of it or the manufacturer can no longer afford to make it. The fall happens **very quickly**.

Examples of Past Fashion Trends

In the early 1960's pant legs were very narrow, but by the mid-1960's a few designers showed wide-legged pants. By the early 1970's everyone was wearing pants with 30″ legs. Then a few daring designers began to show "baggie" pants, full at the top and narrow at the bottom. By the late 1970's pant legs became narrow again.

Length of skirts and the amount of waistline fit cycled greatly during this 20-year period:

1948 Dior's "new look" (fitted waist, mid-calf skirt)

1958 The "sack" or "sacque" dress (without waistline)

1965 The first "mini" looks (with or without waistlines)

1968 the "midi" and "maxi" lengths (with waistlines)

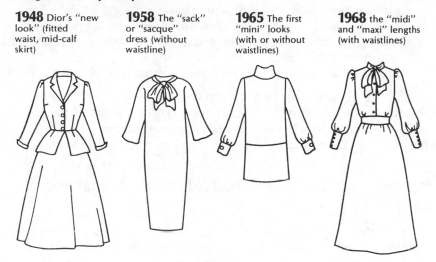

Can you predict the length of a fashion trend? It's been said that if you've worn it in your lifetime, you won't want it again. It takes the next generation to accept an old look that's new to them.

Fashion used to cycle in 10 to 20 years, but the world is moving faster today and people are willing to change more quickly. We are exposed to international fashion influences immediately with television, movies, and printed media. Maybe this is why almost any skirt length is **in** right now. People are having more fun with fashion and feeling more confident about being individual.

Fads Vs. Classics

Both fads and classics have a place on the fashion curve.

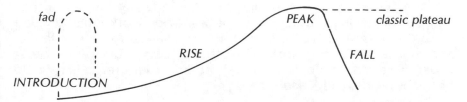

Fads — styles that are short-lived. They rise very quickly to their peak and then fall very quickly. If a fad really catches on, like jeans or down vests, it can turn into a fashion trend. Jeans started the whole western influence. The acceptance of down vests inspired a whole new outer and active wear industry.

Some fads will rarely become fashion trends. They are the ones with:
- gimmicky details like non-functional pockets or buttons.
- bright, "loud" colors like chartreuse or iridescent orange.
- glaring prints using bold colors and high contrast color combinations.
- exaggerated details like very wide, curiously shaped collars.

Classics — styles that satisfy such a basic need that they remain in fashion indefinitely, like the blazer jacket or crew neck sweater. Classics change, but the changes are very subtle. Blazer lapels may get wider or narrower and shirt collars may get larger or smaller.

Use the Fashion Curve to Help You Buy at the Right Time

Like ocean waves, each fashion look curves, crests, and crashes at different rates. As pattern designer Susan Pletsch says, "When you see everyone wearing it at the supermarket, it's headed for the crash!" That is, of course, unless it's a **classic**.

Now think about the fashion curve in terms of making wardrobe decisions that will be good investments, wearable over a long period. Any item that's at the crest of the curve is one that you won't be able to wear as long as one that is a rising trend. In other words, if you buy or sew a style that everyone is wearing now, (other than the classics), chances are it's at the peak and will be out of fashion before it's worn out, or before you've recouped your investment in money or sewing time.

Sometimes we just don't get around to adding a new look as soon as we would like and it's already peaked on the fashion curve. Or, we spot a look we like, but know it's just a fad. If you add it to your wardrobe, you'll have to accept the fact that you must be able to afford to toss it in 6 months or less.

We generally don't sew fads. We would rather invest our time and energy sewing classic pieces, the wardrobe workhorses that last season to season. If we do sew them, we use less expensive fabrics and choose a color that works with other pieces in our closet in order to get more wear out of them in a short time. Our preference would be to buy fads ready-made, on sale!

Looks That Last

Investing your money and time in classic styles is one of the best ways we know to build a season-spanning investment wardrobe. When these pieces are carefully planned in terms of style, color, and fabric, you'll get more than your money's worth in wear and at the same time build some identity and continuity into **your** look.

Classic clothes are no-nonsense, no-frills pieces that withstand influence from fads and trends. They are usually designed with simple, clean lines that put you in control and allow you to cope with continuing style change. Classics are the old reliables, always comfortable no matter what else is on the fashion forefront. They are sometimes even featured in fashion.

Classics give you more for your money when they are done in neutral colors. Also, the higher the quality of the fabric used, the longer wearing they will be and the more chic they will look. Linen and wool are examples of classic fabrics. We'd both rather own a 100% linen suit in classic lines, and have our less expensive linen look-alikes in more casual, unlined jackets.

Fashion often plays on the classics. Don't be fooled. These are TRUE classics and will last the longest:

Classic Styles

(Some are featured in fashion right now — others are waiting their turn.)

Shirtwaist dress (one or two-piece)
Classic cardigan jacket (V or round neckline)
Standard blazer
Shawl-collared blazer
The Chanel suit
The "costume" — simple straight dress with matching jacket

Turtlenecks
Convertible collar and bow blouses
Menswear-style shirts
Crewneck and V-neck Shetland and cashmere sweaters
Simple cardigan sweater
Fitted, straight-legged pant with fly front zipper
Trouser, skirt or pant (straight-legged)
Dirndl skirt (40" - 50" around bottom)
Kilt

Classic Details

Set-in sleeves
Medium-width sleeves gathered into blouse cuffs or pleated into shirt cuffs
Hems just below the knee

Medium-width lapels and collars on jackets
Straight medium-width sleeves on jackets

9

Do Your Fashion Homework

Looking is Free

When styles change, we "snoop shop" to get ideas for new color stories and design details. Snoop shopping will save you time by whittling down your fashion choices. Looking is free (not to mention fun!) and it will help you decide what to sew or buy.

Shop Magazines First

To get a fashion overview, read fashion magazine editorial features and fashion ads. Subscribe, or purchase pre-season issues in August and September, and again in January and February.

We recommend **Vogue, Harper's Bazaar, Mademoiselle, Glamour,** and **Self.** We also enjoy "W", a bi-monthly newspaper condensation of the fashion news that appears in **Woman's Wear Daily,** the fashion trade publication for designers and buyers. (Address on page 127.)

The European fashion magazines like **L'Officiel** and the French and Italian editions of **Vogue** and **Bazaar** are generally one or two years ahead of American fashion. They provide good information for forward dressers.

Don't forget pattern company fashion magazines such as **McCall's Patterns Magazine** and **Vogue Patterns Magazine.** They not only show the newest fashions but give you lots of fabric information.

Get a Fast Fashion Education with Magazines

When you read fashion magazines, remember that much of what is featured is the most extreme example of what's to come. By the time it reaches the majority of stores, it will be toned down and more acceptable to the average person.

To quickly spot fashion trends, read a magazine by flipping through the pages checking only **one** detail at a time. If you are interested in trends in hem lengths, look **only** at hems in all the ads and fashion pages. Look through the magazine again noting only shoulder widths and sleeve styles, then again only looking at collars and necklines. You will have learned much more in the same amount of time as going through it once very carefully.

Be A Fashion Clipper

Clip out new looks and tape them to your closet door. Live with them for awhile to get used to them. People often react negatively to new styles ("I wouldn't wear that to a dog fight!") because their eyes haven't adjusted to the newness yet.

Pay special attention to accessories and how they are worn and trends in hair styling shown with the fashions. A change in clothing style often **requires** a change in hair style to balance the look.

Snoop Shop Before You Buy

"Snoop shopping" means to look in better stores for the things you've seen in magazines, but leave cash, checks, and credit cards at home. There are **two** kinds of snoop shopping:

1. **Just looking** in order to develop an overview of fashion trends for each season.
2. **Trying on** new looks you like to see how they look on you. Take with you: a tape measure, a small notebook, and your prettiest face and hairstyle. Wear something easy to remove in the dressing room and comfortable shoes. (Bring a dressy pair along also, as the wrong shoe can spoil a great look.)

First, Just Browse

Look through the store to see what it has to offer, paying particular attention to the following:
- window displays and mannequins.
- how the store accessorizes new looks
- what makes something look "now" instead of last year

Now Try On

You can and **should** try on anything that catches your eye because of color, details, or design lines. Don't let price tags discourage you. That's the fun of snoop shopping!

Even try experimenting with colors and styles that don't appeal to you. You might be surprised. It's your chance to try on all those designer clothes and luxury fabrics you've never dared try before. Be brave! Critically evaluate what you see by standing as far away from the mirror as possible to get the full effect.

How Does It Look?

- Do the design lines accentuate your assets and draw the eyes away from your liabilities?
- How does the fabric look and move on your body?
- Is it a good color for you?

What is Good Fit? Check the Following in the Dressing Room

Neckline hugs base of neck without wrinkling or gaping.

Bust darts point to, but stop within, 1" of bust point.

Blouse front doesn't gap at bustline.

There is "wiggle room". Room for two fingers in waistband.

You should be able to "pinch an inch" of fabric at your fullest hip in fitted skirts and pants.

Jacket shoulder is ¼"-½" wider than blouse shoulder.

Blouse sleeve is set in at your pivot bone. Raise arm straight out to side and the bone you feel moving is your pivot bone.

Waistline curve or seams are at natural waistline.

Jacket sleeve length reaches wristbone and allows for ¼" to ½" of blouse to peak out. (Coat sleeves are ½" longer than jacket sleeves.)

Can you move freely in the garment? Bend arms and lift them over your head. Remember, however, to make fitting room calisthenics relevant to the clothes. You won't be wearing a blazer to play basketball.

Take Notes

When you've found some things that look good on you, make notes on the following in your notebook:

- name of store should you want to buy the garment
- interesting fabric or color combinations for future reference
- fiber content
- price (to help you determine whether to buy or to sew)
- names of designers you like for future reference
- interesting construction techniques to use if you sew
- measurements of best jacket lengths for new skirt and pant looks
- measurements of flattering hem widths and sleeve and skirt lengths

Also note why something didn't look good, so you can avoid it in the future. And sketch interesting styles or accessories for future purchasing or sewing. These notes will help you plan the best fashion looks for you.

Dressing to Suit Your Style

By developing your own clothing style, your clothes will say to everyone who sees you, "I'm comfortable. I'm confident. I know who I am, and I'm happy with how I look."

You will also be able to sew or buy with confidence even though there are many new choices each season. You will easily be able to pick the one new idea that is **you**.

Clothing Style is developed after you have analyzed the following:

Personal Style — Who you are. What image do you want to project?

Lifestyle — What you do. What clothing do you need for your activities?

Bodystyle — Your size and shape. What fashion lines and details will create the illusion you want?

Colorstyle — The colors that bring out your best features. Which ones are most enhancing to your personal coloring?

Have you ever tried to identify these styles in yourself? Read on and we'll show you how!

Personal Style

Two women can put together the same basic wardrobe pieces, but because of their "personal style" they will look different.

If you take time to identify your personal style, you won't be a slave to fashion, jumping from one look to another. Your clothing choices should reflect who you are and how you feel about yourself.

What are you most comfortable wearing? How do you want other people to describe the way you look? Your answers to these questions should help you identify and define your personal style.

If you had money for only one outfit, which of these four looks would you choose? Circle it.

A

B

C

D

You've probably chosen the one that reflects your dominant personal style, the one that should be reflected in your wardrobe. If you chose:

A . . . Your look is **Tailored**.
B . . . Your look is **Romantic**.
C . . . Your look is **Sporty**.
D . . . Your look is **Dramatic**

You may be any one or a combination of these four personal styles, but it will save you time and money to stick to one style, your dominant personal style, for your basic wardrobe. Clothes for evening and sports activities are an easy way to break out of your normal image for a change. Also, accessories are a way to incorporate your secondary style. For example, if your look is mostly tailored, but you have some dramatic flair, a dramatic piece of jewelry on your tailored blazer will make the statement you want.

Lifestyle

The way you spend your working and personal time is what makes up your lifestyle. Each stage you go through, whether in school, working at home, outside the home or doing volunteer activities, creates certain changes in your lifestyle. Some activities remain constant while others will be added and others discarded over time.

Every so often, stop and analyze how you spend your time. Then buy or sew **only** the clothes that work for your current activities. If you do, you'll never have to face a situation and say "I don't have a thing to wear!"

We are all dreamers and it's easy to select clothes for the lifestyle they promise instead of letting our lifestyle determine the clothes we select. In other words, no matter how great it looks on the model, it really doesn't pay to sew a vampy red evening dress if you have no occasion to wear it.

The following are the common lifestyle stages. Where are you now?

- Moving from college to a job
- Young homemaker and mother
- Working mother
- Re-entering the job field
- Professional woman
- Homemaker and volunteer worker

More than half of all American women work outside the home and more are entering the labor force every day. This lifestyle transition creates a big change in wardrobe demands, but it's not only the working woman we want to address. One-third of all American women are full-time homemakers. They need an even more varied wardrobe to meet their hectic daily schedules from childcare to entertaining.

Chart Your Lifestyle

How and where do you spend your time? Once you know this, you can examine your clothing needs in terms of your lifestyle. Take a look at your daily routine using the following chart:

Lifestyle Chart

	HOURS SPENT DAILY							Weekly Total
	Sun.	Mon.	Tues.	Wed.	Thurs.	Fri.	Sat.	
Professional Time								
Full-time work								
Part-time work								
Volunteer work								
Family Time								
Mothering								
Cooking								
Shopping								
Other household activities								
Social Time								
Church								
Entertaining								
Entertainment (dining out, cultural activities)								
Recreation Time								
Sewing								
Arts/Crafts								
Sports								
Sleeping, relaxing								
Other								

Make a Lifestyle Pie

Use your finished chart to determine the percentage of total time you spend in each of the time groupings, then create a visual picture of how you spend your time. This is your **Lifestyle Pie**. For example . . .

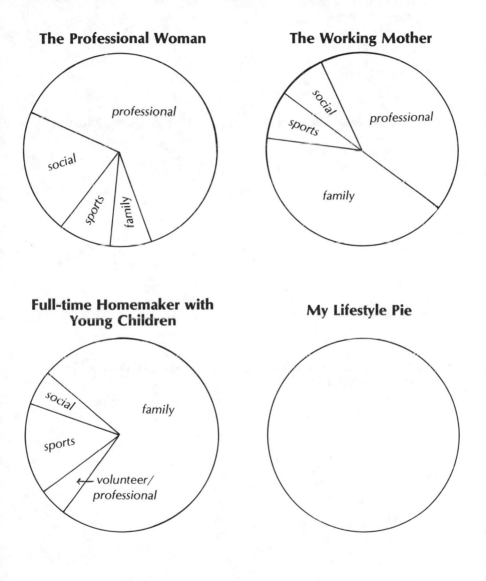

The Professional Woman

professional

social

sports

family

The Working Mother

social

sports

professional

family

Full-time Homemaker with Young Children

social

sports

family

volunteer/ professional

My Lifestyle Pie

Convert Your Lifestyle Pie to a Wardrobe Pie

Each of the activities on your lifestyle pie probably requires clothing in one or more of the following categories:

- Anytime Casuals ("kidproof" if necessary)
- Classic Sportswear
- Career Clothes
- Daytime Dressy
- Evening Dressy

For example:

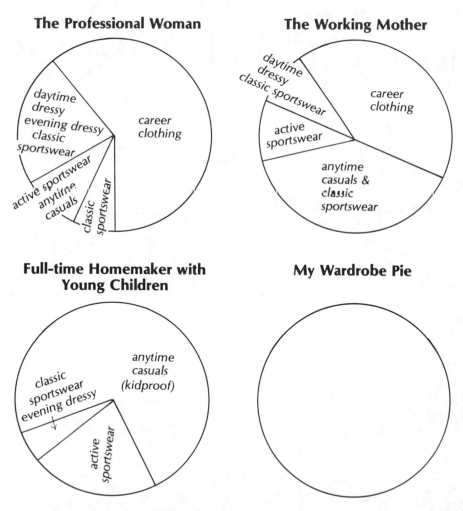

The Professional Woman

daytime dressy
evening dressy
classic sportswear
active sportswear
anytime casuals
classic sportswear
career clothing

The Working Mother

daytime dressy
classic sportswear
active sportswear
career clothing
anytime casuals & classic sportswear

Full-time Homemaker with Young Children

classic sportswear
evening dressy
active sportswear
anytime casuals (kidproof)

My Wardrobe Pie

Ideally, your wardrobe pie should reflect the needs of your lifestyle pie. The size of the slices should be the same. If it doesn't, make it a goal to balance the two.

Bodystyle

Whether you sew or buy, the finished look you create is largely influenced by your bodystyle which has 3 characteristics:

Size — your height and width
Shape — your silhouette
Proportion — the length of your body sections

Make a Figure Graph and a Profile Graph

This is the best way to analyze your figure and to see yourself as others see you. It will only take 20 minutes and the help of a friend! Follow these easy steps:

1. Pin or tape two 6' lengths of 1" squared graph paper (Stacy's Tracer or Pellon's Tru-Grid) side by side on a wall. The bottom edges should be cut even with an uncarpeted floor.
2. Wear non-binding panties and bra. No girdles unless you **always** wear one. Put on a necklace to find the base of your neck and tie a cord around your waist.
3. To make your **figure graph**, mark a lengthwise center line on one paper. Stand in your normal posture with your back against the graph and your body centered on the center line.
4. Have your friend plot your body points as indicated on the illustration on page 20. Keep pencil close to your body and perpendicular to the wall.
5. For a basic diagram of your body, have your outline carefully traced on the paper; or, step away and draw lines to connect the dots. Draw a horizontal line across the top of your head.
6. Take the paper off the wall and fold it in half, half again, and again creasing it into 1/8's. (For the first fold, line up the top of head with bottom of feet.) You have now divided your body into 8 sections.

Note: The perfectly proportioned figure is 8 "heads" tall. That is, the total height is 8 times the measurement of the head and divided as shown on page 20.

7. Now make your **profile graph** on the other paper taped to the wall. Stand in front of it in your normal posture with your side touching the wall. No fair pulling in your tummy unless you **always** do. Have your friend outline your body.

Now Compare Yourself to Perfect Proportions

Top of head

*Shoulder slopes 2"
from neck base*

*Underarm is ½ way
between top of head
and hip.*

*Waist is ½ way
between underarm
and hip*

*Hip (top of thighs)
divides body in ½*

*Hips are 1" narrower
than shoulders for
garments to fall freely
over hips.*

*Knee is ½ way
between hip and feet*

Soles of feet

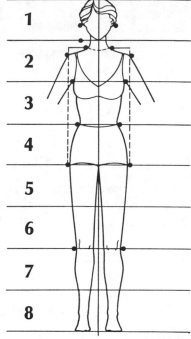

If your . . .

*Shoulders slope ½"
more or less than the
ideal, you are sloping
or square.*

*Waist is more than 1"
above or below the
ideal, you are short or
long waisted.*

*Leg length is more
than 1" longer or
shorter than ½ your
body length, you are
long or short legged.*

Now Draw a Box Around Your Torso (Shoulders and Hips)

Your silhouette is . . .

hourglass	*triangle*	*inverted triangle*	*rectangle*
			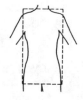

if you have . . .

*balanced hip
and shoulder
width.*

*narrow shoulders
in comparison to
hips.*

*wide shoulders
in comparison
to hips.*

*little or
no waist
indentation*

Record observations from both graphs on the worksheet on page 21.

Your Bodystyle Worksheet

Body Size

HEIGHT ____ SHORT (4'10"-5'3") ____ AVERAGE (5'4"-5'6")

____ TALL (5'7"+)

WEIGHT ____ THIN ____ AVERAGE ____ HEAVY

Body Shape (Silhouette — Use Figure Graph)

____ TRIANGLE   ____ INVERTED TRIANGLE

____ HOURGLASS   ____ RECTANGLE

Body Proportions (Use Figure Graph)

LENGTH

WAIST: ____ SHORT ____ AVERAGE ____ LONG

LEGS: ____ SHORT ____ AVERAGE ____ LONG

WIDTH

SHOULDERS: ____ NARROW ____ AVERAGE ____ BROAD

HIPS: ____ NARROW ____ AVERAGE ____ BROAD

WAIST: ____ NARROW ____ AVERAGE ____ THICK

SLOPE

SHOULDERS: ____ SQUARE ____ SLOPING

UNEVEN

SHOULDERS: ____ LEFT LOWER ____ RIGHT LOWER

HIPS: ____ LEFT LOWER ____ RIGHT LOWER

Profile (Use Profile Graph)

BUST: ____ SMALL ____ FULL ____ AVERAGE

____ LOW ____ HIGH ____ AVERAGE

TUMMY: ____ FULL ____ FLAT ____ AVERAGE

DERRIERE: ____ FULL ____ FLAT ____ AVERAGE

Colorstyle

When you wear a color that is right for you, your personal coloring comes alive. Your skin glows, your eyes are bright, and your hair is filled with highlights. The wrong colors can overpower and drain, casting gray shadows that emphasize under-eye circles and dull your hair and eye colors. Worst of all, the wrong color can be **aging**. (Oh NO!)

Facts About Color

1.	Color is the first thing your eye sees.
2.	Color is free with every garment you buy or sew. Buying the best color costs no more than buying a not-so-great one.
3.	Color can influence your emotions and those of the people around you. For example, red is energizing and green is calming.
4.	Colors build confidence when you know they are personally enhancing.

Finding Your Best Colors Saves Money

• The closet of the average American woman represents a minimum investment of $2,000. Knowing your best colors guides that investment in the most positive direction.

• Knowing your best colors reduces impulse buying and eliminates poor choices based on personal reaction to color.

• Color knowledge broadens your skills in combining colors and helps you find new combinations already in your closet.

• Knowing your best colors creates consistency in a wardrobe and causes lots of "happy accidents" — things just seem to go together!

3 Ways to Find Your Best Colors:

1.	**Color analysis by a trained color consultant** — These people use a variety of systems:

• **Color by season** — individuals who share common characteristics are grouped into the four seasons: Spring, Summer, Fall, Winter.

• **Color key method** — individuals are placed into Key 1 (cool, blue skin undertone) or Key 2 (warm, yellow skin undertone) groups.

• **Composite method** using a combination of the above with personal body colors, body build characteristics, and bone structure.

Knowing your "season" is not as important as knowing your best colors and how to use them. Choose a good color consultant but remember, color consultants are human. They are limited by their personal perceptions and even they can have a bad day! A good consultant would offer to redo your colors if you just aren't comfortable with them.

How Can I Choose a Color Consultant?

Investigate the following:

• **Individual vs group sessions:** Group sessions cost less and you learn by watching others. Individual sessions result in more personalized attention to your hair, skin, and eye coloring.

• **Number of color swatches:** You'll be given 20 to 30 colors in group sessions, and 150 to 200 in a personal analysis.

• **Are additional services available?** Having your colors "done" is almost useless without instruction in how to use them. This should be included in the basic fee. Many color consultants are also qualified to help with wardrobe planning, personal shopping, figure analysis, and make-up instruction.

• **The best lighting for color analysis:** Natural daylight from a northern exposure is best because it doesn't cast harsh shadows or reflect any color of its own, or the color consultant may use a color-corrected daylight lamp.

• **The cost:** As with anything, you get what you pay for. Consultants charge as little as $10 and as much as $300. The consultant who charges a very low price may not have the qualifications to provide good service.

2. **Color analysis by the book** — This is a great way to heighten your color awareness. Most books set up guidelines to help you determine your correct color category. Most include color charts but color reproduction is **very difficult** to control and can be deceiving. Some books provide an address for mail order color swatches. In many cases, the cost of the book plus swatches is equal to personal consultation.

3. **Do-it-yourself color analysis** — It can be done but it is really difficult to be objective. Here are some tips to help you decide which colors are best on you.

• **Pay close attention to what people say.** Unsolicited compliments like, "You look terrific!" are usually given because the onlooker is reacting to the positive effect of a color on you. However, if they say "Wow, that's a gorgeous color!" they are often reacting to the color, and not to its effect on you.

• **Look in your closet.** What colors are your "old reliables"? What colors are the things you never wear?

• **Test for your best colors.**

1.   Go to a fabric store. Wear a neutral color (preferably off-white) that won't interfere with colors you are testing.

2.   Take a selection of solid color fabrics to a mirror by a window. Take colors you like and ones you don't like or don't think look good on you. You might have some pleasant surprises!

3.   Drape each color across your front and over your shoulders. Don't focus on the fabric, but concentrate on your face and what happens to it with each color change. Discard any samples that:
   - Cast a gray shadow on your face
   - Deaden your eye color
   - Make any wrinkles, blemishes or facial discolorations (like ruddiness) more obvious

4.   Decide your skin undertone. Hold up a yellow/red fabric, then a blue/red. Does one look better on you? Now do the same with a yellow/green and a blue/green.
   blue based colors best = cool skin (Summer or Winter)
   yellow based colors best = warm skin (Spring or Fall)

5.   Gather the colors that have worked best for you and buy 1/8 yard of each. This is just a beginning. As you find a new enhancing color, add it to your collection.

Start Wearing YOUR Colors

It can take 3 to 5 years of conscious effort to develop a wardrobe that is totally color-keyed to your personal color palette, so be patient! If everything in your closet seems wrong, don't try to change it all at once. Here's how to begin:

1.   Wardrobe additions should be in your colors.

2.   What you wear closest to your face counts the most. If a suit is the wrong color, add a blouse in the right color. If a dress is the wrong color, wear a scarf the right color next to your face.

3.   If you are simply not comfortable in a color recommended by your group or color consultant, don't wear it. You have to **feel** good in order to **look** good.

4.   The clothing you wear at home should be flattering to you also. You'll feel happier and more energetic — and accomplish more!

5. Should you wear a color **not** recommended by your color consultant? If it makes you feel terrific, your personality and positive attitude will overcome any color negatives.

Shop With Your Colors

1. Don't leave the house without your colors! You never know when or where a fabulous bargain will appear!

2. Check colors in daylight, since flourescent lighting can distort color. If daylight isn't near, take the item to the nearest window.

3. When buying a print, hold the piece up to you and stand 3 feet away from a mirror. The dominant color (the one with the most impact, not necessarily the background color) will stand out and that must be enhancing to you.

4. When trying a color you've never worn before, try it in a small investment, close-to-the-face piece, like a scarf, blouse, or sweater.

Organize Your Colors So They Are Easy to Use

• Mount small swatches on index cards. Assemble them in a clear plastic wallet photo holder. It is important to remove the color from the plastic to compare to a garment.

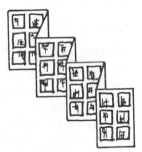

or

• Make a fan out of clear acetate strips. Attach small fabric swatches with double-faced masking tape.

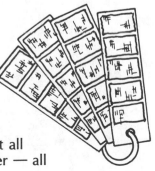

• Group your colors so that all colors in one family are together — all reds on one stick, for example.

• Be sure to have your name and address on each card or stick. Your colors can be expensive to replace!

Your Color Groups: What They Mean and How to Use Them

Neutrals — the Wardrobe Workhorses

Neutrals act as backdrops for your personal coloring and wardrobe colors. The true neutrals are black, white, and gray. Colors can be neutrals too:

beige	*navy*	*teal blue*
brown	*forest green*	*plum*
burgundy	*olive green*	*mauve*

Finding Your Best Neutrals

- Of all neutrals, black, white, gray, beige and brown are the easiest to work with. The others may take more careful planning, but are often more interesting.
- Neutrals can be warm or cool. Use the ones with the same undertones as your skin.
- Your most flattering neutrals will be ones that repeat part of your personal coloring — hair, skin or eyes. The **best** repeats your natural hair color.

Combining Neutrals

Dressing head to toe in neutrals can be boring. Avoid monotony by using at least two of the following to create interest:

- contrasts in light and dark
- interesting texture someplace for visual appeal
- interesting print or fabric design
- interesting, unusual, or dramatic design line.

About White

- White should not be worn in large quantities unless you have lots of contrast in your coloring like dark hair and light skin.
- White is difficult to wear close to your face because it can drain the color from your skin, causing blemishes, lines, and shadows under the eyes to show more. Avoid white when you are tired.
- White demands attention. Small amounts worn close to your face will distract the eye from a color that is not so good for you.

Eye Color: Look really closely at your eyes — most people have at least 3 colors and some as many as 20. The composite color of your eyes, seen best from 3 feet away, is one of your most effective wardrobe colors. Your eye color is a comfortable, trusting color.

Dramatic Colors: Complementary colors (those opposite each other on the color wheel - see below) enliven each other. For most people, blues and greens are their dramatic colors because they enhance the orange and red-orange in the skin.

Dramatics can be worn head to toe, or used to add a spark of color to neutral outfits. Attention to detail in grooming is a must when you choose dramatic colors since they draw all eyes towards you! Don't wear them when you'd rather **not** be seen or heard!

Red: Everyone can wear red — it emphasizes the femininity in women and the masculinity in men. If you have a warm skin tone, wear yellow-reds; if your skin tone is cool, wear blue-reds.

Reds are high energy and can be overpowering when you are tired, bringing out dark circles under your eyes! Softened shades of red, like pinks, are better for those times. Red is the most romantic color and it intensifies other people's reactions to you. Don't be afraid to wear it, just choose the occasions when you know you can handle anything!

Elegant, understated colors: If you take away your dramatic colors, your reds, your eye colors, and your neutrals, you are left with your elegant, understated colors. If you are ever in doubt about what color is appropriate for an occasion, select one from this category. You will always look attractive in these colors, but you won't stand out like you do in dramatic colors and reds.

The Color Wheel

The color wheel gives us a picture of the relationships of the 12 basic colors and helps us to use color more effectively.

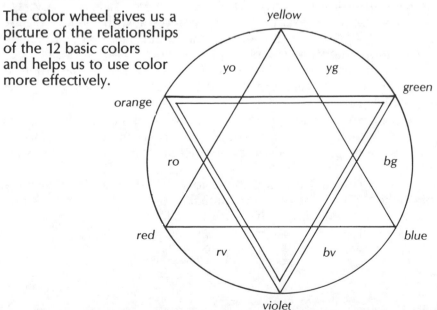

Primary colors — red, yellow, blue — are the colors used to mix all other colors on the color wheel.

Secondary colors — orange, green, violet — are mixtures of two primary colors.

Tertiary colors — red-orange, yellow-orange, yellow-green, blue-green, blue-violet, red-violet — are mixtures of one primary and one secondary color.

Make the Color Wheel Work for You

Hang a color wheel on your closet door to remind you to use more color and more interesting color combinations in your dressing.

General combination guide: Use a major amount of one color (a suit), a minor amount of a second (a blouse), and just a dash of a third for an accent (a scarf). Equal amounts create a spotty appearance.

The easiest (and safest) color combinations:
• Neutrals, head to toe.
• A neutral with a color accent (blouse or accessories).
• Monochromatic — an outfit in variations of one color, like a burgundy suit, pink blouse, and a dark burgundy print scarf.
• A multicolored print with any of the colors in the print.

More interesting color combinations for the adventurous:
• **Analogous colors.** The two colors to the left and to the right of each color are analogous or related colors. If you choose blue-green, its analogous colors are green and yellow-green to the left, and blue and blue-violet to the right. Add a maximum of 2 analogous colors to your main color. For example, wear a green suit with a yellow blouse and a yellow-green silk flower on the lapel.
• **Complementary colors** — These colors are opposite each other on the color wheel. They are best worn in unequal amounts since they intensify each other so much. Accessorize a yellow dress with violet.
• **Split complementary colors.** The two colors on either side of the complementary color are the split complements. Accessorize your yellow dress with red-violet or blue-violet for a more interesting look.
• **Triad colors.** These are the colors linked by a triangle on the color wheel. They are the most difficult combinations to work out, but the most interesting when done well.

blue-green	blue	blue-violet	violet
yellow-orange	red	red-orange	orange
red-violet	yellow	yellow green	green

Clothing Style

You can look smashing, no matter what size and shape you are. Accept your basic body structure, because no amount of exercise or dieting can change your frame. Learn to make the best choices in clothing styles for your bodystyle. Three elements of design are your tools for drawing attention to your best features and de-emphasizing your not-so-good ones.

Line — The eye follows line. Usually, vertical lines add height and horizontal lines add width. Line also divides spaces, and can be used to change proportions.

Color — The eye is first attracted to light colors, bright colors, and warm colors. Use these to emphasize your best features.

Texture — Fuzzy, tweedy surfaces add bulk. Smooth surfaces take off weight. Dull surfaces recede, making you look smaller; shiny surfaces reflect light, making you look larger. Shiny surfaces also attract the eye, so you can use them to frame a pretty face like wearing a satin blouse under a flannel blazer.

Use Line to Your Advantage

There are 2 types of lines that make up the total look of a garment:

Outside Lines *silhouette*

Inside Lines *seam lines, hem lines, decoration lines, and lines in patterned fabric.*

Outside Lines

Use outside lines or silhouette to create the illusion of the shape you would like to be.

To determine the silhouette of a fashion, stand at a distance and squint. Which shape do you see? Or draw a line around the outside of a fashion photo in a magazine. Which shape did you draw?

Fashion examples of the 4 basic clothing silhouettes:

Triangle   **Inverted Triangle**   **Hourglass**   **Rectangle**

Creating Illusion with Outside Lines

(Refer to your Bodystyle Worksheet, page 21)

You can wear any silhouette as long as you can get it to fit; however, some will emphasize your best features better than others. The guide below should help you evaluate clothes you consider buying.

If your body shape is:	These silhouette shapes would . . .			
▲	. . . hide hips.	. . . widen shoulders to balance hips, but hips may require a larger size.	. . . balance hips to shoulders, if waist is small.	. . . balance hips to shoulders, but hips may require a larger size.
▼	. . . emphasize broad shoulders.	. . . balance hips to shoulders, but unflattering if you're short and full.	. . . balance shoulders to hips, but work only with small waist.	. . . emphasize or not fit full bust or broad shoulders.
⧓	. . . emphasize shape — good for small hourglass figure.	. . . focus on shoulders.	. . . fit nicely, but hide best feature of small waist.	. . . emphasize bust and shoulders, but hide small waist.
▮	. . . help create a pleasing shape.	. . . help create a pleasing shape.	. . . hide thick waist.	. . . emphasize thick waist.

Inside Lines

Inside lines are the hardest to see in a garment, so train your eye to see them using our tracing technique. Place tracing paper over the photo. Trace the lines within the garment - seam lines, hem lines, lines created by trim or decoration. Will the inside lines enhance your figure?

- Which lines dominate, horizontal or vertical?
- Are horizontal lines placed at desirable areas you want to enhance?
- Are the diagonal lines long or wide?
- Are there softening curves?

Creating Illusions with Inside Lines

Vertical lines

lead the eye up and down to lengthen and narrow.

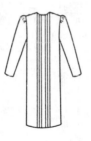

Horizontal lines

lead the eye across and widen. They have the most power to hold the eye, so avoid placing them at unflattering positions.

Curved lines

have the same effect as the vertical or horizontal to which they are closest. Very full curves add roundness to the figure giving illusion of more weight. The curves in this blouse widen the shoulder and add fullness to bust.

Diagonal lines

lengthen or shorten depending on their slope.

These widen torso.   *These lengthen body.*

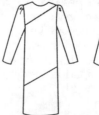

31

When Lines Interact

Most designs are composed of many lines. When lines interact, their usual effects are altered. For example:

When a vertical line is interrupted by a horizontal line, it loses some of the heightening effect.

A vertical line will look even shorter if another line forces it downward.

When the vertical line becomes the magic Y, as in this V-neckline, it creates an even greater illusion of height.

Two vertical lines placed close together are more slenderizing and lengthening (a) than if placed far apart (b). Then the eye travels **across** the body.

When two or more horizontal lines are used together, the widening effect is stronger than if only one is used.

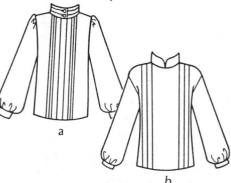

a

b

Even spacing of stripes that are the same width and color value will reverse the principles above. Then you get **both** a widening and heightening effect. Here your eye climbs them like a ladder adding height as well as width.

Create the Ideal Change Proportion

The "ideal" proportions (the relationship of your parts to each other — especially the lengths of each body section) are ones that are uneven. The ancient Greeks claimed that a 1/3 to 2/3 ratio is the most aesthetically pleasing division of spaces. The following are examples of lines dividing clothing spaces.

Dividing the space in half is uninteresting.

Two ways to create the Ideal Proportion

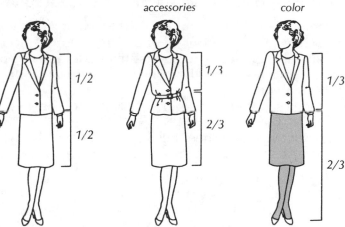

accessories   color

Use Lines to Change Your Proportions

A dropped waistline conceals a short waist.

A raised waistline conceals a long waist and gives the illusion of longer legs.

If your legs are long you can wear the longer jacket, which also conceals a short waist.

A shorter jacket gives the illusion of longer legs.

Hems Are Lines That Can Change Proportion

The hemline of most garments is a horizontal line that should stop at a point:

- flattering to your body
- pleasing in proportion
- close to the current fashion length.

You can always shorten or lengthen any garment a little to make it closer to **your** best length and proportion and still appear fashionable. **To determine your best length for skirts, dresses and coats:**

1. Stand before a full-length mirror in the height shoes you wear most often. Hold fabric in front of you draped to the floor.
2. Gradually raise the fabric to several different locations on your leg. Notice as you move the "hemline" up or down, your leg will look thicker or thinner.
3. Find 3 lengths flattering to your overall proportion — one near the knee, the calf and the ankle.
4. If you wear a variety of heel heights, try this exercise again with different shoes, since heel height affects your leg shape and your proportion.

A good, safe length for most is the "shadow" of the knee where the calf curves in toward the back of the knee. However, the fuller the style, the lighter the color, the softer the fabric, the shorter **or** longer skirts can be. In narrow shapes, darker colors, and heavier fabrics, it is best to keep the length closer to the calf curve.

Jackets

Jackets should be either long enough to hide the derriere or stop somewhere above the fullest part of the hip. When a jacket stops at the hip, it emphasizes width. Consider overall proportion and the following as well:

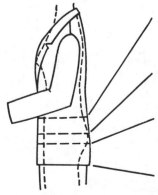

Short jackets — best with skirts or well-fitted pants of the same color.

Above fullest part of hip — OK for thin hips and short people.

Just below fullest part of hip — best length if jacket is to be worn with both pants and skirts.

Well below fullest part of hip — hides hips best. Safest length for average to tall people or those with very long legs.

Pants

Fashion usually dictates pant lengths. The narrower the leg, the shorter the pant must be.

However, regardless of fashion, the longer the pant leg, the longer your legs will look. Pants should be as long as possible without breaking on the front of the shoe. Shoe heel height drastically affects the pant length and overall appearance. Try on pants with shoes you plan to wear with them.

Narrow legs must be shorter in length.

Straight legs can touch top of shoe in front.

Wide legs can go to the floor.

Make cuffed pants as long as possible since the horizontal lines visually shorten.

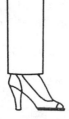
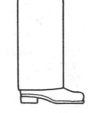

Shorts

The shape of your leg will determine the best length and style. Experiment by pinning the hem in different positions.

Avoid a length that hits you at the fullest part of your thigh.

Fuller legs make your legs look smaller.

Curved sides will make your legs look longer and thinner.

Walking shorts with full legs are a good cover-up for too-thin or too-full legs.

Use Color to Create Your Best Illusion

Light colors advance and can be used to increase apparent body size.

Dark colors recede and can be used to decrease apparent body size.

Bright and warm colors advance and are most easily seen. Use them to emphasize or increase body areas.

Dull and cool colors recede and are less visible. Use them to camouflage or de-emphasize body areas.

Use Texture To Create Your Best Illusion

Texture is the look and feel of fabric. Wear heavily textured, bulky, crisp, or shiny fabrics where you want to enlarge or draw attention. The smaller and shorter you are, the lighter, softer and more drapeable the fabric should be. Full figures should avoid the bulk of heavily textured fabrics and revealing sheers. Middle of the road is best, or use soft fabrics in fuller styles.

Texture	Fabric Examples	Effect
Soft, drape well	Tissue faille, chiffon, lightweight wool gabardine, challis, Ultrasuede® brand fabric, Ultrasuede® Facile™, wool jersey	Drapes softly over curves; slimming in loose styles
Soft and clingy	Single knits, silk jersey, charmeuse, crepe de chine	Tend to follow body curves more closely
Moderately crisp	Dress weight linen, eyelet, double knit, poplin, heavy gabardine, pique, wool flannel, Ultrasuede® brand fabric	Stand away from the body and flatter most figures because they don't cling
Very crisp	Suit weight linen, voile, taffeta, heavy denim, satin	Stand away from the body and enlarge the figure
Bulky, coarse, rough, fuzzy	Tweeds, fur, heavy flannel, sweater knits, velours, wide wale corduroy	Enlarge the full figure and dwarf the very small unless nap is short
Smooth	Broadcloth, crepe de chine, gabardine	Flattering to the figure
Shiny	Satin, charmeuse	Reflect light, increase body size
Dull or matte	Matte jersey, flannel, challis	Absorb light, figure looks smaller

Make the Most of Your Bodystyle With the Right Clothing Style

Each of our bodies vary from the "ideal" figure in different places. Don't think of these variations as problems. Take into account your total silhouette and your problems may have little effect on it.

If in doubt about a new look, go to a store and try it on. If you are in a fabric store, hold fabric up to you draped in the shape of the new look. When considering a certain design or pattern, note where your eye goes first. This focal point should be at one of your best features. It can also be used to draw the onlooker's eye away from your figure variations.

The following summarizes the use of line, color, and texture to counter your extremes. Remember, there are exceptions to every rule.

If you are . . .

Short — Create heightening vertical design lines such as those found in single-breasted jackets, V-necklines, and trouser pants. Monochromatic outfits will lengthen your look as will neutral shoes, hose or boots that match the hem of skirt or pant legs.

Wear higher heels, upsweep hair styles, and shorter skirts. Long skirts will shorten and overpower you. Keep prints small and accessories simple in scale.

Tall — Lucky you! However, overusing lengthening lines could make you look like an undernourished giraffe! You can break your height with tops of one color, bottoms of another. Sweeping styles like capes, longer, fuller, flared skirts, and full coats add grace to your figure. Full tops are great if you have long legs. Longer jackets are best for you.

Accessories can be dramatic — chunky jewelry, wide belts, and luggage-style bags. Your height would be exaggerated with the contrast of small prints, delicate ruffles, and tiny buttons.

Heavy — Use vertical lines and one color dressing to coax the eye up rather than across. Medium to dark colors are most flattering, but be careful with black. It can make a large body stand out in contrast to lighter surrounding. If heavy in one area only, use dark colors there and light elsewhere. Create a focal point near your face.

Wear shoes with a heel height of at least 1" for the most graceful look. Use softer fabrics for flared and A-line skirts and for layered looks. Avoid oversize prints, design details and jewelry. Medium scale is best.

Thin — Wear textured and heavy fabrics unless you are very short, then in moderation. Yokes, gathers, tucks, ruffles, wide sashes, and pockets are enhancing details. Blouson styles and full, tiered skirts add weight. Stay away from too many vertical lines, clingy fabrics and dark hose.

If you have . . .	These looks will flatter . . . (see dictionary next page)
Broad Shoulders	Raglan, dolman, dropped shoulder sleeves. V, U, scoop necklines. Shawl, convertible, wing collars. Halters, strapless tops. Ascots, neckties, jabots. Tent silhouettes, full skirts.
Narrow Shoulders	V, square, bateau necklines. Small collars. Set-in sleeves. Extended or padded shoulders. Cap, puff, leg-o-mutton sleeves.
Square Shoulders	(Same looks flatter as for broad shoulders).
Sloping Shoulders	Padded shoulders, yokes. Set-in sleeves.
Small Bust	Scoop, cowl, halter necklines. Any neckline focus. Empire waistlines with fullness above seam. Ruffled, tucked or softly draped blouses. Vests, short, shaped and bolero jackets.
Full Bust	Shallow V-necks. Shawl, convertible and open collars. Soft, pretty shoulder details. Blouson, A-line, shift and shirtwaist styles. Long sleeves. Cardigan and Chanel jackets.
Short Waist	Contour or narrow waistbands. A-line, shift, princess silhouettes. Blouson and dropped waistlines. Overblouses, tunics.
Long Waist	Wide belts, fitted waistbands rather than contour. Short jackets, vests, sweaters. A-line, shift, empire styles. Full gathered skirts. Below knee skirt lengths.
Short Neck	V, U, scoop, square necklines. Open collars. Camisoles, cardigan jackets, long chains.
Long Neck	Bateau, keyhole, cowl, funnel necklines. Turtleneck, mandarin, tailored shirt, and high Victorian collars. Ruffles, bows, scarves and jewelry at neckline.
Heavy Arms	Bishop, peasant, dolman, kimono sleeves. Short sleeves that don't hug the upper arm. Loose fitting jackets layered over tops.
Thin Arms	Cuffed shirt, bishop, leg-o-mutton and other full sleeves.
Broad Hips (full thighs and/ or derriere)	Tent, empire, A-line shirtdress. A-line, gored, flared bias and wrap skirts. Loose fitting straight-cut pant. Tunics, long, shaped jackets, blouson tops.
Narrow Hips/Thighs	Gathered, dirndl, hip-stitched or fully pleated skirts. Shorts, pants, trousers, jumpsuits, culottes, harem pants. Overshirts.
Flat Derriere	2-piece dresses with a gored skirt. Skirts and pants that are pleated or gathered at the waist. Split skirts, culottes, harem pants.
Full Tummy	Dirndl skirt with soft gathers or pleats mostly at the side. Overblouses, tunics, box-style jackets. A-line skirts with soft inverted front pleats.
Thick Waist	Dropped waists, A-line, shift, tent silhouettes. Jackets worn open.
Short Legs	Raised waistlines. Straight-legged pants. Narrow skirts. Shorter jackets and sweaters. Higher heels.
Long Legs	Tunics or long sweaters. Mid-calf length skirts. Tiered skirts. Ankle length pants.

Your Fashion Dictionary *(See Chapter Ten for additional fashion terms.)*

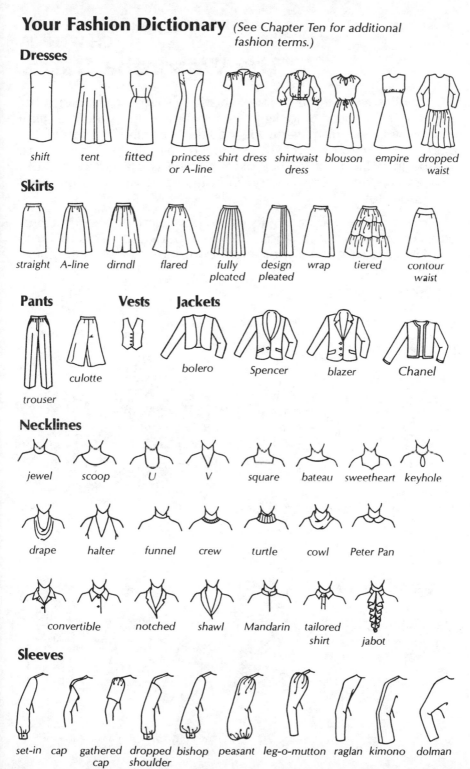

Dresses

shift | tent | fitted | princess or A-line | shirt dress | shirtwaist dress | blouson | empire | dropped waist

Skirts

straight | A-line | dirndl | flared | fully pleated | design pleated | wrap | tiered | contour waist

Pants

trouser | culotte

Vests

Jackets

bolero | Spencer | blazer | Chanel

Necklines

jewel | scoop | U | V | square | bateau | sweetheart | keyhole

drape | halter | funnel | crew | turtle | cowl | Peter Pan

convertible | notched | shawl | Mandarin | tailored shirt | jabot

Sleeves

set-in | cap | gathered cap | dropped shoulder | bishop | peasant | leg-o-mutton | raglan | kimono | dolman

The Wardrobe Basics

Building a wardrobe is easier when you start with the basics. For a maximum number of looks from a minimum investment of time and money, we plan wardrobe additions around 5 coordinated pieces. You may discover that some or all of these pieces are already in your closet. If they haven't given you a variety of looks (at least 6), your pieces are too individual and weren't purchased as coordinates.

Having basic wardrobe pieces in classic designs need not produce a boring "uniform" look. Choose fabrics and colors suited to your personal style and buy or sew a few trendier styles to add spice.

5 BASIC PIECES

3-piece matched suit in a solid, neutral color; choose your most flattering styles

2-piece dress (blouse with tie and skirt) in a print that coordinates with suit

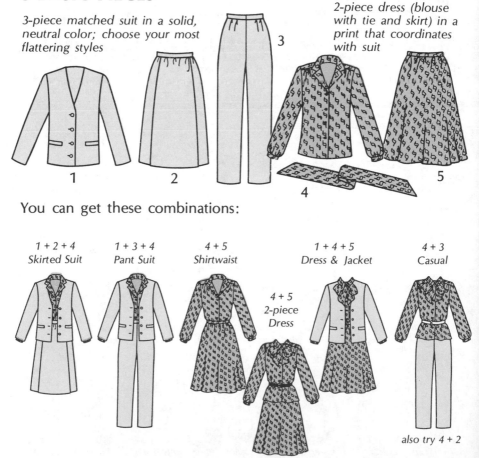

You can get these combinations:

| 1 + 2 + 4 | 1 + 3 + 4 | 4 + 5 | 1 + 4 + 5 | 4 + 3 |
| Skirted Suit | Pant Suit | Shirtwaist | Dress & Jacket | Casual |

4 + 5
2-piece
Dress

also try 4 + 2

Expanding the Basics to Create Your Wardrobe Core

The addition of just three carefully planned pieces has a multiplier effect creating **many more** possibilities.

Add another blouse or shirt in a solid color that will work with the 2-piece dress and the 3-piece suit.

Mix in another 2 or 3-piece suit that will work with all 6 pieces. Choose a solid color or a subdued tweed for the versatility.

6

6 + 2   6 + 2 + 1   6 + 3   6 + 3 + 1   6 + 5   6 + 5 + 1

7   8

7 + 4 + 2   7 + 4 + 5   7 + 6 + 2   7 + 6 + 3   8 + 6   8 + 6 + 7

Selecting the Basics

- A suit represents the largest dollar investment to buy and the largest investment in time and money to sew. Every woman can benefit from owning at least one good suit. Even if suit dressing isn't your style, the pieces can give great variety in unmatched, casually coordinated looks. Suits should make a positive fashion statement and work harder and wear longer than anything else in your closet.
- Buy the best quality in fabric and workmanship that you can afford.
- Start with a 2 or 3-piece matched suit in a neutral color that you can build on or one that coordinates with suits or separates you already own.
- Suits trimmed or piped in a second color are limited in their wardrobe multiplying possibilities.

Now, Which Jacket to Choose?

1. A single-breasted jacket is almost always more slenderizing than a double-breasted style. Double-breasted jackets add visual pounds with their wider lap and draw the eye across the figure shortening it. If you want a double-breasted jacket, look for one with two buttons at or just below the waist and with a narrow wrap so you can wear it casually open as well as buttoned.

2. Classic cardigan jackets work with almost any kind of neckline in blouses and dresses, and with most skirts and pants.

3.   A blazer is a versatile type of jacket that can form the top of a suit for work, be at home with casual pants, or be worn with dressy separates for evening, depending on the fabric you select.

4.   Jackets that last from year to year usually have simple set-in sleeves. Image Consultant Emily Cho cautions us to be wary of "one shot" jackets — those that have shapes or details that limit their mix and maximize ability. Save trendy styles like pleats, tucks, gathers and exaggerated shoulders for those fun items that add spice and variety to your wardrobe. Here are examples of one-shot jackets:

5.   When choosing a jacket to wear with many different bottoms, consider both the jacket length and the width around the hips. Full skirts require a jacket fuller in hips or shorter in length. Slim skirts and pants work with a longer, slimmer jacket.

About Skirts and Pants

You will get more wear out of your jacket when it has two bottoms — two skirts, two pants, or one of each. For example, select one to match the jacket and the second in a coordinating fabric. Or, choose both in the **same fabric and color** as the jacket but in **different styles**, for example, one straight skirt and one flared.

Or, if you wear out pants first, make two pair exactly the same. If you have small children, make one pair that's kid-proof, and make the other in a dressier fabric.

Two-Piece Dress Virtues

1.   Two-piece dresses add versatility and long life to any wardrobe plan. When pulled together with a belt, they look like dresses but their separate parts mix with other things too.

2 pieces + belt = same look of a belted 1-piece dress

2.   Two-piece dresses might take more time to sew than a one piece, but they are easier to fit because you can buy the blouse pattern in one size and the skirt in another. In ready-to-wear, two-piece dresses are often available as separate pieces.

3.   You will get even more fashion mileage if you choose a print for your two-piece dress. Small to medium-sized, classic prints in subdued colors are the most versatile. They can often be worn with other prints, subdued tweeds, and plaids. If they contain one or more neutral and one or more accent colors, they automatically will mix with more.

4.   Softer fabrics, more feminine blouses and soft skirts help to add variety to the crisper look of tailored suits.

Blouse and Shirt Options

1.   Blouses receive the most wear and since they will need to be replaced more often, they are the best and least expensive place to play with fashion trends — new sleeve details, interesting collar or neckline treatments, new-to-you colors.

2.   Blouses with a finished straight bottom edge (rather than shirt tails) can be worn out and belted as overblouses for a definite two piece look. They can also be tucked in and belted for a shirt dress look.

4. Blouses with convertible shirt collars or standing band (Mandarin) collars are more versatile than those with other necklines. It's easy to dress up both styles by adding matching scarves, ruffles, detachable collars, or bows. (See pg 59.)

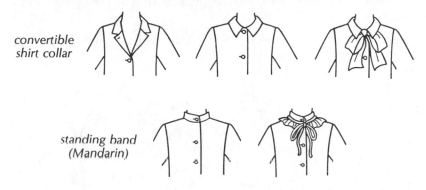

convertible shirt collar

standing band (Mandarin)

5. A blouse or shirt with a detachable self tie gives you more wearing options for the money — wear the scarf as a soft bow, looped into a casual scarf, or tied or wrapped around the waist as a belt.

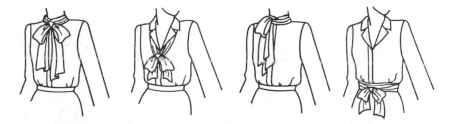

6. Deep kimono and dolman sleeves and dropped shoulder blouses are often awkward to wear under a jacket. Extremely full sleeves will be crushed under jackets and often unattractively sag below the jacket sleeve. We reserve these for skirt or pant plus blouse looks.

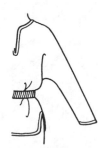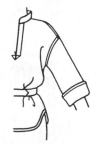

full sleeve   boxy kimono style   deep dolman   dropped shoulder

Add Versatile Pieces

The eight pieces in the expanded basic wardrobe add up to wardrobe versatility in any fabric from denim and corduroy to wools, linens and sophisticated silks. However, you may want to add some of these pieces for even more fashion variety:

Sweaters can change the mood and the season. Choose a cardigan for one more "jacket" look with other pieces.

classic crew or v-neck   turtle neck   sweater vest   cardigan

Feminine blouses in lace and ruffles soften the suit look for daytime occasions and pretty evening transitions.

Camisoles change skirts into sundresses, daytime suits into evening ensembles, and double as "slips" under sheer blouses.

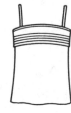
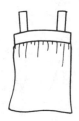

T-shirts in cotton knit mix with jeans, pants, every day skirts. Try dressier T's in wool or silky jersey to team with a matching skirt for a new twist on two-piece dressing.

Casual pant styles add comfort in easy-care fabrics, or go dressy in wool crepe or silk.

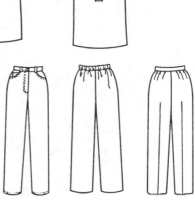

Tunics and wraps stand alone or double up over blouses, pants, or skirts for day, at home, and evening.

Pullover dresses in easy knit shapes add comfort and seasonless dressing options, and are especially great for travel.

Warm Winter Coats

In addition to choosing a dense, tightly woven warm fabric, and an insulating lining (button or zip-in liners make rain coats and storm coats more season-spanning) look for these details for keeping off the winter chill.

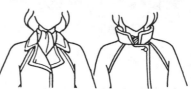

high cut collars/necklines or collars that convert to buttoned-up looks

oversize collars to wear up or detachable hoods

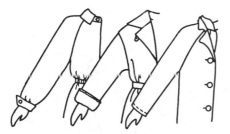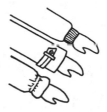

roomy cut, especially in sleeves, to allow for layering over jackets and bulkier sweaters; deep armholes, or raglan sleeves

sleeves with adjustable tabs, drawstrings, or snug inner knit cuff to keep out the cold

belts to wrap in body heat

long enough to extend over boot tops at least 1" after being belted

flaps or plackets covering front buttons or zippers

What to Do About Evening Wear???

1. Use accessories and fabrics to change an outfit from desk to dinner:
    • A silk or silky blouse is dressier
    • Wool gabardine or crepe are dressier than tweed or corduroy
    • Classic pumps or sling back shoes are dressier

2. Collect pieces that can turn your daytime basics into exciting evening costumes.

3. Splurge on a fabulous dress that makes you feel wonderful and wear it to all your special occasion events.
4. Wear your prettiest lingerie — it will make you **feel** special!

The Best Fabrics For Your Wardrobe

Develop Fabric Savvy

Because we all live in different areas and have different lifestyles, there is no single "best" fabric. But if you know some basic fiber and fabric facts and some specific advantages and disadvantages, you should be able to select the best fabric **for you**. Be sure to read the labels on ready-to-wear and on the end of the fabric bolt for your best overall guide to fiber content and care.

Fiber and Fabric Facts

1. **If in doubt about fiber content, burn a small snip** from a seam allowance or fabric yardage over your bathroom sink. Generally, if it leaves a soft ash and/or smells like burning hair, it is a natural fiber. If the residue is hard and brittle, it is synthetic. Acetate is easy to identify; it will dissolve completely in acetone.
2. **Fiber absorbency is a clue to wearability and durability.** The **more absorbent** fibers are more comfortable to wear because they absorb body moisture and humidity. Since they absorb moisture, they are less prone to static electricity and will clean more easily. The **less absorbent** fibers are less comfortable to wear, but since they are less affected by body heat and moisture, they wrinkle less and hold their shape better. However, they become static-prone and some will pill more easily.

Where does your fabric fall on the Absorbency Scale?

More absorbent ◄————————► **Less absorbent**

wool linen silk cotton	rayon acetate acrylic nylon polyester
natural fibers	synthetic fibers

3. **The length of a fiber affects its performance and appearance.**

Long fibers are mainly synthetics. Silk is the only natural long fiber, but there are longer wool and cotton fibers that have some of these characteristics. They are:
* smooth and lustrous
* wrinkle resistant
* pill resistant
* more resilient

Short fibers are natural and synthetic fibers cut into short lengths and twisted into a yarn that has a fuzzier appearance. They are:
* soft and fuzzy
* tend to pill
* wrinkle more easily

Wool gabardine is an example of a long fiber fabric, wool flannel a short fiber fabric.

4. **Manufacturers use blends for many reasons**, such as to decrease cost, increase prestige, increase washability, decrease wrinkling, increase comfort, or increase strength. 35% of a fiber in a fabric is needed to make a difference (except for prestige!), 50% to get the most out of that fiber's best qualities.

A shirt of 65% cotton, 35% polyester will wrinkle less and wear better than an all cotton shirt. A shirt of 65% polyester, 35% cotton will wrinkle less and wear better, but be less comfortable. The trend today is toward a combination of comfort and easy care rather than 100% easy care.

These fibers added to a fabric...	Will result in...
Cotton or linen	Increased absorbency and comfort, less static build-up, better dyeability.
Wool	Added bulk and warmth, Increased absorbency, increased shape retention and wrinkle recovery.
Silk	Luster, luxury, comfort.
Mohair	Added strength, loopy texture, added luster.
Cashmere and camel hair	Added warmth, luxury, improved drapeability, soft smooth texture.
Angora rabbit hair	Softness, fuzziness.
Acrylic	Improved softness, wool-like qualities.
Rayon	Lower cost, better absorbency, lower static build-up, added luster.
Nylon	Increased strength, abrasion resistance, wrinkle resistance, lower cost.
Acetate	Improved drapeability, more luster and shine, lower cost.
Polyester	Wash and wear qualities, wrinkle resistance, shape retention, durability, lower cost.
Spandex	Elasticity and comfort.

Blends can change the care instructions. For example, a wool can become washable if polyester is added. If you are not sure of the care instructions, care as you would for the most sensitive fiber.

5. **Finishes can change the characteristics of a fabric.**
Soil Release — helps fabrics to release dirt and oil-based stains more easily. Visa, Fantessa, Zip Clean, and Zelcon are brand names.
Permanent Press — helps fabrics wrinkle less, require less pressing, but has a greater tendency to attract oily stains and to pill.
Water Repellency — causes water and stains to run off fabric surfaces rather than be absorbed, but fabric can still get wet with long contact with water. Scotchgard and Zepel are brand names.

6. **Fabric weave affects durability and appearance.**

 **Plain weave:** Each yarn runs over one and under another in both directions, producing a strong firm fabric. Fabrics can be of all weights — chiffon, gingham, canvas, flannel, challis are examples of this most common weave.

 Satin weave: Float yarns pass over several crosswise yarns to produce very lustrous, shiny fabrics. These long yarns can easily be caught and cause snags. Charmeuse and satin are examples of this fragile weave.

 Dobby and Jacquard weaves: Figurative designs are woven into the fabric. Dobby designs (birdseye and pique, for example) are usually small, geometric figures. Jacquard designs (damask, tapestry, brocade) are more complicated and can be quite large. Both are expensive to produce and can be fragile if there are large areas of long float threads.

 Twill weave: A diagonal parallel rib is formed in this weave. It is the most durable weave of all. It is strong, resilient, wrinkle-resistant, and often soil-resistant due to the yarn density. Examples are denim, gabardine, silk surah, and calvary twill.

Knits: a series of interlocking loops instead of yarns that cross each other at right angles. Knits are durable, comfortable because they give, and are subject to only an occasional snag. There are both single knits (tricots and sweater knits) and double-knits (interlocks and traditional doubleknits).

Shopping Tips for the Savvy Seamstress

1.   Wool and wool blend tweeds are the fastest to sew because they hide sewing mistakes and press and mold to shape easily.

2.   Solid colors are faster to sew than plaids, prints are faster than either as the print in the fabric doesn't require matching and will camouflage any mistakes. Plaids are the biggest time taker of all because of the cutting concentration and planning required.

3.   Carry this handy chart with you when shopping. Fill in the yardage required for your 5 Basic Pieces. Just use the handy yardage conversion chart in the back of the pattern catalogues if your fabric width is different.

---

5 Basic Pieces Yardage Requirements (45" fabric)

Jacket _____	Jacket lining _____
Pants _____	Jacket interfacing _____
Skirt _____	(most are 22")
Blouse _____	Buy same amount of lining as
Matching skirt _____	fabric for pants and skirts.

How Can I Tell if This Fabric Will Work For Me?

You can make some tests on both ready-made clothing and on fabric that will give you some clues. We can tell you how to decide if a fabric will wrinkle, but you must decide if that will keep you from buying.

1. **Test wrinkle resistance and recovery.** Crush a corner of the fabric in your hand and release. Do the wrinkles stay or fall out quickly? If the wrinkles don't fall out, the garment will look unpressed and rumpled. The higher the natural fiber content, the more it will wrinkle. We call these natural fiber wrinkles "status wrinkles" when the fabric is expensive. Wovens wrinkle more than knits, stretch wovens wrinkle less than regular wovens.

2. **Check wearing qualities and shape retention.** Stretch the fabric between thumbs and forefingers and hold for 5 seconds. If the yarns shift or slip apart easily, strain on the seams could be a problem at stress points. If there is no yarn shifting and the fabric springs back, it will hold its shape. The tighter the knit or weave, the heavier the fabric, and the less absorbent the fiber, the better it will hold its shape. Generally, wovens hold their shape better than knits, and synthetics better than natural fibers.

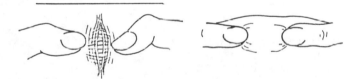

3. **Test the fabric for a tendency to "pill".** Fabrics made out of short fibers are more likely to pill. Take an inconspicuous corner and gently rub the right sides together; if this produces slight balls or pills, this will also happen in abrasion areas on your clothes such as the underarm and pant crotch. The less absorbent the fiber, the drier and more static-prone the fabric will be; therefore, the short fibers will cling together and pill more easily.

4. **Look at the fiber content for a comfort guide.** Check our absorbency scale (see page 50) and compare it to your fabric fiber content. In general, fabrics that are lightweight and high in natural fiber content are more comfortable to wear. Synthetics are often warm and feel clammy because they don't breathe or absorb as well as natural fibers. However, they will wrinkle less.

5. **Grainline should be accurate in fabric and ready-to-wear.** The print on a fabric should follow the woven threads, and the lengthwise and crosswise threads should be perfectly at right angles. If not, the fabric will not hang properly and if you sew it will be difficult to cut.

Whether you are buying fabric or ready-made clothing, you should invest in the best quality you can afford for your 5 Basic Pieces. These coordinates need to be durable and make you look like a million! Follow our fabric suggestions for the appropriate fabric.

Fabrics for Matching Skirt, Jacket, and Pants

Fabric	Advantages	Disadvantages
Wool Gabardine	Made from long wool fibers that are highly twisted. Tightly woven with a smooth surface. Wears extremely well. Comfortable, as wool fibers breathe and insulate. New lightweight gabardines are seasonless, hold their shape well, wrinkles hang out. Dry-clean only.	Shows press marks easily so use a press cloth. Cleaners can also easily overpress, so request careful pressing. Expensive.
Polyester Gabardine	Made from texturized yarns, so is wrinkle-resistant. Polyester is very durable. Washable. A year around fabric except in hottest and coldest climates. Always looks crisp and fresh.	Close in appearance to wool gabardine, but not quite as rich looking. May snag or pill. Will be less comfortable to wear than wool, as polyester is cold in winter and warm in summer.
Linen	Irish linen is top quality, those made in Poland and China wrinkle more. Generally wears well, never pills. Very comfortable as fiber is extremely absorbent. Dark colors or neutrals are seasonless fabrics. Dry-clean (linen is washable but hard to iron).	Loses body after many cleanings. Spray on fabric finish (sizing) to restore crisp feel. Dark colors may show wear (on cuffs, hem folds) more quickly than lighter colors because of the dyes used.
Linen-like	Choose heavier weights for better wear and more wrinkle resistance. These blends wrinkle less than real linen. Blends include rayon, polyester, cotton, linen. Less expensive than linen, can also be a year round fabric in dark or neutral colors. Washable or drycleanable.	May pill. Loses body after washing or drycleaning. Generally not as durable as real linen, nor as rich in appearance.

For more information on tailoring a blazer or suit jacket, or on sewing and fitting pants, see page 128 for ordering information for these Palmer/Pletsch Books — **Easy, Easier, Easiest Tailoring** and **Pants for Any Body**

Fabrics for 2-Piece Dress (Matching Skirt and Blouse)

Fabric	Advantages	Disadvantages
Polyester crepe de chine	Drapes beautifully. Can have fullness without bulk. Wrinkle resistant, very durable, machine washable. Some types will breathe better than others — open weaves and loosely woven fabrics will be more comfortable.	Pretreat oily stain before washing. Remove from dryer immediately to prevent heat setting wrinkles and puckered seams. Very tightly woven types are not absorbent and will feel clammy.
Silk crepe de chine	The original that many synthetics copy. Drapes like no other fabric, feels wonderful, relatively comfortable in all climates. Most manufacturers suggest drycleaning, but can be washed, (see page 114 for instructions). Prints and dyes beautifully. Many different weights and types from which to choose	Expensive. Must hand wash or dry-clean. Perspiration can damage fibers and stain. Wrinkles, so loosely fitted garments are suggested to minimize wrinkling.
Silk Broadcloth	A sportier, more shirting-like fabric that wears better than crepe de chine. Often available in shirting stripes, plaids, gingham, also solid colors. Hand washes nicely. Less expensive than crepe de chine.	Doesn't drape as well as crepe de chine. Wrinkles, perspiration can damage fibers and stain.
Cotton or Blended Broadcloths	More casual than fabrics above. Washable, usually inexpensive. More comfortable than polyester; wrinkles less than silk. Blends include cotton, polyester, rayon.	Doesn't drape as well as crepe de chine. Those with higher cotton content will wrinkle more, higher polyester content will make less comfortable.
Wool or Wool Blends	Soft, lightweight, drapeable, generally printed. Those with wool should be dry-cleaned, some blends (cotton, rayon, polyester) may be washed. Usually has a soft, warm, brushed surface.	Wool is more expensive to buy and to care for, but most durable. Polyester increases tendency to pill. Generally a cool weather fabric.

For more information on sewing with silk or silky fabrics or for speedy sewing tips, see page 128 for ordering information for these Palmer/Pletsch Books: **Sensational Silk**, and **Mother Pletsch's Painless Sewing**.

Fabrics for the Expanded Wardrobe Core: Jackets, Pants, Skirts

Fabric	Advantages	Disadvantages
Wool Tweed, Flannel, Wool Blends	Those with hard finishes and tight weaves will wear best. Tweed is very easy to sew, coordinates with many different wardrobe items because of the multicolor effect. Flannel is a good wintertime basic, comes in medium and light weights for all climates. Blends (wool, polyester, nylon, acrylic) are usually lighter weight, lower in price, some are washable. Dry clean 100% wools.	Generally for winter season only. All can be expensive. Flannel wrinkles more than wool gabardine, looser weave and fuzzier surface won't wear as well. Blends won't wear as well as 100% wools. Some blends will pill. All can be scratchy.
Wool Knit, Jersey	All weights give so are comfortable to wear. Warm in winter. Drapes well in lighter weights, tailors well in heavier weights. Knits are easiest fabrics to sew! Dry-clean.	Expensive. Can snag more easily than a woven fabric. Lack crispness required for fine tailoring. Will stretch out of shape during wear but can be pressed back to shape.
Polyester Knits	All weights are wrinkle-resistant, travel well. Wear well. Machine washable. Hold their shape. Inexpensive.	Like all polyesters, can be warm in summer and cold in winter because fiber does not breathe. Pretreat oily stains before laundering, remove from dryer immediately.
Corduroy, Velvet, Velveteen	Napped fabrics have very rich color and texture. Can be sporty or dressy, depending on type. Some are washable (including washable velvet!) others should be professionally cleaned and pressed. Inexpensive.	Can show press marks and wear lines easily, not very durable. Require special sewing techniques. Wrinkle easily, will stretch out of shape during wear, but will recover shape during washing or dry-cleaning.
Ultrasuede® brand fabric	Elegant and extremely durable. Versatile; comes in 2 different weights for many types of garments. Machine washable, easy care. Holds shape during wear, can be seasonless, depending on color. Sews easily.	Very expensive. Requires special, but easy to learn, sewing techniques. Because it is partially polyester, it will be warm in summer but not as warm as 100% polyester.

For more information on sewing with Ultrasuede® brand fabric, see page 128 for ordering information for **Sewing Skinner Ultrasuede® Fabric**.

Accessories Complete The Picture

Accessories are the details that change the fashion beat each season; they are little things that make a big difference. They are great wardrobe extenders because they create the illusion that you are wearing a different outfit every day. Variety is the spice in dressing and accessories provide that spice. Use them to:

1. Revive or update classics and old standbys.
2. Make a quick change from a day to evening look or from business to casual.
3. Add color and life to neutrals.
4. Focus attention wherever you want it.

If you sew you owe it to yourself to invest some of the money you save in the best accessories you can afford. Good accessories in classic styles are always in fashion. It is better to spend less on faddish pieces that are really just "throwaway chic."

We place accessories in two categories — major and minor. Budget for the major pieces first. Then decide if you can afford (or save money by sewing) some of the minor pieces.

Major (indispensable)		Minor (frosting on the cake)		
shoes	fine jewelry	costume jewelry	scarves	shawls
hosiery	leather belts	pocket hankies	hats	gloves
bags		flowers	fabric belts	

Shoes

Footwear must be comfortable! Leather is the best investment for comfort and durability. Shop in the middle of the day — feet are smallest in the morning and often swollen in the evening.

Considering the cost of better leather goods, your selections should work with most everything and be in harmony with the mood of your clothing and with the shape of your leg.

The Best Shoe Styles and Colors

1. Cleo, our fashion coordinator friend, says that if you can only afford to buy **one** good shoe, make it a closed toe pump in taupe. Taupe is a neutral seasonless color that will blend with everything, and a pump is a style that can be worn with both skirts and pants.

2. A 1½"-2" heel is flattering to most legs. Wear a minimum of a 1" heel if you are heavy, short, or have short legs. Avoid a T-strap shoe, if you have thick ankles.

3. The lower the top of the shoe and the more instep that shows, the longer your leg will look.

4. The more foot that shows, the less business-like the shoe will be. However, a pump with open toes or a sling back might be more comfortable. In that case, a closed toe, sling back pump is more appropriate in professional situations.

5. If you must go from office to evening, a small toe opening in a pump would be acceptable.

Boots

Simple, classic boot styles in quality leather with a medium heel are usually the best investment. Neutral colors (brown, black, burgundy, or camel) are best. A classic black boot is easiest to dress up or down. Burgundy is another good choice because it blends with both black and brown. There should be no gap between the top of your boot and your hem.

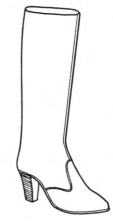

Evening, Casual, and Play Shoes

Add these to your wardrobe according to your lifestyle and your climate. Here are some classics:

Evening	Casual	Play
Strappy pump	*Walking shoe*	*Sport shoe*

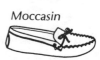

Satiny pump	*Loafer*	*Moccasin*

Strappy flat sandal	*Espadrille*	*Ballet slipper*

Hosiery

The best hose color is one that is a shade darker than your skin. However, using color and texture variations, hosiery can be an inexpensive fashion update or help season-spanning wardrobe basics reflect seasonal change. Your bodystyle will determine what is best for you. Keep the following in mind:

1.   When hose, hem and shoes all match, the lengthening effect is greatest. Or make sure at least your hem and hose **or** your shoes and hose match.

2.   Very dark, very light, and very bright colors as well as patterns and textures draw attention to your legs.

3.   Keep leg coverings in the same mood and weight as your shoes.

4.   The higher the shoe heel and the more open the toe, the more sheer your hose should be.

Belts

Every wardrobe needs belts, minor investments for major results. They are an inexpensive way to update wardrobe pieces, and they can be used to change shape or proportion.

simple chemise

belted to define the figure and create a focal point

belted and bloused

belted and bloused deeply to change proportion and length

Belt Basics:

- ¾" to 1¼" leather belts are fashion classics worth collecting in a variety of colors.

- Belts that match or blend with the color of your clothes are less distracting than contrasting belts, and they give the illusion of a longer line. However, matching belts are less interesting.

- Wider belts are more comfortable to wear in soft materials. They also generally require a taller body, but you never know until you try.

- We look for our best belt buys on sale. Shoe repair shops can inexpensively punch holes or reposition buckles on too large or too small bargain belts.

- Recycle a favorite belt buckle. Shoe repair shops can remove it from the old belt and easily attach it to a new one.

Easy No-Sew Belts

Select several narrow cords or braid trims in complimentary colors and knot them every 6". Buy enough of each to wrap around your waist twice and tie in a knot.

Wrap an unusual cording or wide belting around your waist and tie in a square knot. Wrap around twice for a more important look.

Tie up an evening look with a wide taffeta or velvet ribbon. Finish the raw ends with a dab of Fray Check, a liquid nylon that coats raw edges and prevents raveling. (See page 95.)

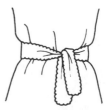

Add an elegant touch to a simple outfit with an Ultrasuede® brand fabric belt. Buy a 2" or 3" width (it's 45" wide) and just wrap around your waist.

Ultrasuede doesn't ravel, so the edges can be left raw or scallop them with scalloping shears.

Bags

- It's no longer a rule that your bag must match your shoe, but matching will simplify things.
- Neutral colors (black, brown, tan, taupe, burgundy) are the best investments.
- Leather is best for year round use.
- Neutral colored canvas, linen, and straw bags for spring and summer work with any color shoe.
- Make sure it will hold your normal contents. Leslie empties the purse she is carrying into the one she is considering to check capacity before buying.
- A shoulder bag is convenient. Be sure the strap is short enough for the bag to hang at the top of your hip bone. If it hangs at your full hip or midriff, it will make those spots look wider. Longer straps can be worn diagonally across the body and still end at the top of your hipbone. Purse snatching has made this style popular world-wide.

- Another classic is the handbag style. If long enough, straps can be worn over the shoulder when carrying a lot or for safety.

- Envelopes and clutches are dressier looking and ideal for the business woman to slip into a briefcase. Inset gussets prevent the overstuffed look.

- The best evening investment is a black fabric clutch.

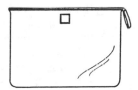

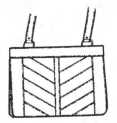

Briefcases

- Choose a briefcase in quality leather that matches or blends with the color of shoes you wear most often. The darker the leather, the more expensive the look. Burgundy is a versatile choice.
- A leather tote bag is a practical alternative to the briefcase. Although not as formal, totes hold more.

Choose from these basic styles:

Classic Structured   *Softer Shape*   *Envelope*   *Tote Bag*

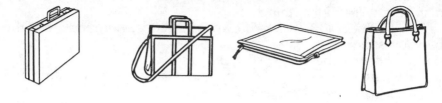

 • Consider two briefcases — a quality leather for fall/winter, and a lighter colored canvas or linen for warm weather months.
 • Keep your case in proportion to your size. There is nothing less feminine than looking like an overloaded packhorse!

Briefcase Details that Work

 • Reinforced handles and a removable shoulder strap for easier handling when juggling suitcases on a business trip or for shopping.
 • Double stitching for durability, and corners reinforced with metal clips to prevent early signs of wear.
 • Inner compartments for easy organization.
 • Sturdy clasps or zipper top closure for security.

Jewelry

 • Less is best! A strand of pearls, gold earrings or a special pendant can be worn every day. It simply becomes your trademark.

 • Keep jewelry simple for a classic tailored look. Buy the real thing or good fakes, depending on your wallet. Basics are:

— A pair of simple gold or silver and pearl earrings.
— A strand of pearls.
— One or two fine chains in gold or silver.
— A watch that is compatible with other jewelry.
— A simple gold or silver bracelet.
— A daytime ring.

Other Classic Accessories

Leather Gloves — Silk-lined are easier to slip on. Knitted styles with leather palms are a good alternative for driving.

Hats — Fedora and berets are classics.

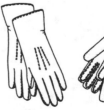

Scarves Can Work Wonders!

Practical and versatile, scarves are a valuable face-framing asset and can create dramatic wardrobe changes. Some scarf selection hints:

1. Oblong (rectangular) scarves are the **most** versatile.
2. Silk scarves can be dyed in clear bright colors. They are also the easiest to tie.
3. Multicolor print scarves will be more versatile and a better investment, because they will blend with more things.
4. Straight-of-grain scarves tie crisper bows than ones cut on the bias and take less fabric if you are going to sew your own.
5. Good scarves basically never go out of style — by investing in scarves you love and following current scarf tying trends you can fashionably use a great scarf for years.

There's More than One Way to Tie a Scarf

Stumped on how to tie or knot your scarves? Some rainy afternoon pull out all your scarves and any square or long and narrow fabric remnants and play with these ideas:

wide to narrow oblong   *square to triangle*

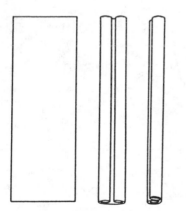

square to oblong

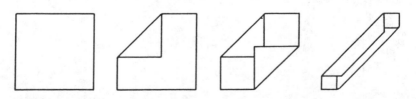

try the classic ascot from an oblong scarf or a folded square

a new angle on the cowboy scarf — tie a square knot (remember Girl Scouts — right over left, left over right) and shift the knot to front, back or side

fill in an empty neckline for a soft splash of color

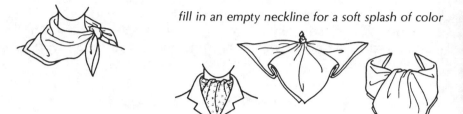

frame your face with a centered knot, then tie at the back

turn a scarf into a "necktie" . . .

or

add dash with the "flip" . . .   or loop the loop . . .   or make a pretty rosette

or a soft stock tie

64

Scarves as an evening top:
Make a large square into a draped
halter — tie at neck and waist
and wear with a favorite jacket.

Scarves as belts:

Wrap once or twice and softly tie; or twist, then tie.

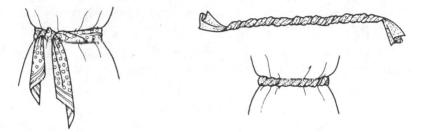

Make a cummerbund from an oblong: start at front, cross ends in back, twist ends, bring forward and tie.

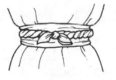

Try a soft sash from two scarves twisted together and knotted at the side.

Loop two long scarves together in front of you. Wrap to the back and tie; or crisscross ends and bring them to the front, tuck under "belt" to anchor.

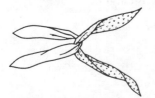
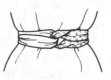

Accessory Rules

1.   If in doubt, don't wear it!

2.   Understatement is always better than overdoing, especially when it comes to jewelry. Concentrate on one body spot — ears, neck, or wrist, but not all three. Take a second look to see if you should add a piece or remove one.

3.   Keep accessories in proportion to your size. For example, too large earrings on a tiny person can be distracting.

4.   If it's the first thing someone else will see when they look at you, **take if off** unless that is where you want to focus their attention.

5.   If a piece is important in size, color, or design, you will need fewer pieces.

6.   You can use accessories to set the tone of your look. For example, you might use a whimsical piece to put a little humor into your appearance.

7.   Remember that accessories are just one small part of your total picture. If you're afraid you've overdone it, remove something before you walk out the door.

Accessory Add-up

One of the tricks many fashion consultants use to be sure they haven't overdone a look will work for you too. When you think you are ready to walk out the door, do some quick addition:

Give yourself 1 point for each of the following:

____ each visible item of clothing
____ each accent color
____ each patterned or textured fabric
____ each decorative trim
____ each piece of jewelry
____ colored nail polish
____ colored toe nail polish (if toes show)
____ colored or textured hose
____ hat
____ handbag (3 points if it is multicolored, has contrasting trim or decorative hardware)
____ exposed hanky
____ contrasting belt (2 points if it is especially ornate)
____ decorative, eyecatching buttons
____ eyeglasses (2 points if ornate or in a fashion color)

If your total is over 14 points, you are probably overdressed. Remove or change something to bring your total down. The result will be a more pleasing unified appearance.

Sew Easy Accessories

Use accessory notes and sketches from your snoop shopping trip, try one of the pattern company's accessory pattern packages, or try our favorites.

Our Favorite Bow From Only 1/8th Yard of Fabric

1. Cut a strip of fabric 4½" × 45".

2. Fold strip in half lengthwise, right sides together and stitch a ¼" seam along the raw edges. Leave a 2" opening in the center.

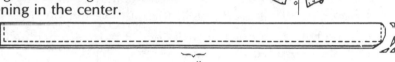

3. Trim corners. Turn and press.

4. Form narrow neck section by folding in half lengthwise and stitching the two edges together for 14" in the center as shown.

5. Turn right side out and press, centering seam.

Lace Ascot or Bow

Two pieces of scallop-edge flounce lace (available in 18" to 36" widths) pieced at the center back will tie into a soft bow or ascot (depending on lace width).

1. Buy ¼ to ½ yard and cut in half crosswise.

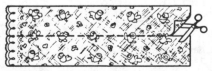

2. Seam short edges at center back, finish long edges with narrow hem.

Detachable Self Fabric Ruffle

Barbara loves the way this changes the look of a blouse with a Mandarin collar, and Leslie used this trick to give a silk T-shirt an evening look.

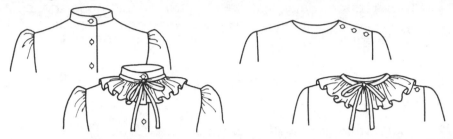

1.   Cut a strip of fabric for ruffle along the selvage 3½" wide and twice the length of your neck measurement. (Selvage edge will become finished outside edge.) Snip mark the center on raw edge.

2.   Finish the two short ends of ruffle with a narrow machine hem. Machine baste raw edge at ⅜" and ⅝".

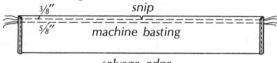

Draw up basting so gathers equal neckline measurement, less ½".

3.   Cut bias strip 2" wide and 1½ yards long. Snip mark center back on long edge.

4.   Pin ruffle to bias strip right sides together, matching snips. Adjust gathers and stitch ⅝" from edge.

5.   Flip ruffle up out of way. Fold bias strip right sides together. Stitch ends and long edges up to ruffle.

6.   Turn raw edge under and slipstitch.

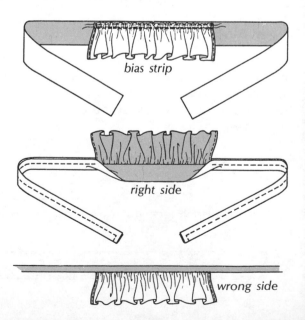

Closet Cleanout

Take Stock of What You Have

"No matter how many things I make or buy, I never have anything to wear!" Does this sound familiar? Wouldn't you like to spend half the time acquiring half the clothes, and still end up with twice as much to wear? Wardrobe organization can make a better investment of your shopping and sewing time. It begins with your closet.

It's often difficult to part with clothes, especially when you have made them yourself. But when you give up a garment that no longer looks or feels good, you are giving up something that no longer supports or enhances you, and making room for something that will.

Make closet cleanout a seasonal habit. Do it early each season — August for the fall/winter and March for spring/summer. This way stores will have the best selections of things to fill in the fashion gaps.

Style your hair and put on your make-up — you will be trying on **all** your clothes and nothing will look good if you look awful.

Ready, Set, Toss!

1.   Pull **everything** out of your closet and drawers. If you live in an area where seasonal clothing is needed, put away those items that won't work for the coming season.

2.   Try on **everything**. You can't tell how something looks by just holding it up to yourself. Be sure to try on the right shoes and undergarments with each item.

3.   Evaluate each garment using the chart below:

How often did I wear it this year (season)? _____

	Yes	No	Maybe
1. Design lines are appropriate to my bodystyle.			
2. Fits well.			
3. Can be altered to fit if necessary.			
4. Style is attractive.			
5. Color is enhancing.			
6. Fabric is in good condition (worth keeping).			
7. Style is still fashionable.			
8. Can be updated or worn a different way if not currently fashionable.			

4.   Divide the clothes on your bed into 3 categories: the "keepers", the "sleepers", and the "losers".

The "Keepers" — clothes you love to wear, the ones with the most checks under the "yes" column. If any of them need minor repairs, put them in a separate pile labeled "Fix it NOW" (or "replace it NOW" if it's something you adore but it's just plain worn out!). The keepers will become the foundation of your new wardrobe plan.

The "Sleepers" — things with the majority of checks in the "yes" and "maybe" columns. They might not be currently fashionable but are good candidates for updating. They are not sleepers if the fabric is worn or of poor quality. Their value doesn't warrant your time or the cost. If the item failed the color test but passed everything else, don't toss. We make old favorites we've sewn or expensive purchases work with the right color scarf at the neck or by adding a new blouse in our best color.

We never toss sleepers until we have exhausted their possibilities as parts of a new look. Use the "scarecrowing" technique on page 72.

"But it Might Come Back into Style!"

Don't let your awareness of the fashion curve get the best of you. There is a rise and fall in the life of most fashions, but it's not always repetitive. A fashion can come and go and come back again; but it seems that fashions never come back quite the same. Besides, most of us don't have the luxury of a large room for a closet like our fashion coordinator friend, Cleo, so we just can't keep everything!

According to **Glamour Magazine**, these items

Will never come back:	**Will always come back:**
Shoe styles	Most wool sweaters, regardless of
Handbag styles	length, neckline, and fit
Popular prints	Knee length skirts
Giant collars, lapels or	Anything classic in a very good fabric:
exaggerated cuffs	leather, suede, cashmere, silk
	Belts

The "Losers" — garments with 4 or more "no's" and items you rarely or never wear. Note any consistencies. For example, if you've tossed lots of square necklines, remember to avoid them in the future. If you find this pile bigger than what remains, take consolation in the fact that you're not alone. Most women wear only 10% of what is in their closet.

If you're not sure whether something should be kept, ask yourself, "Have I worn this in a year?" If not, chances are you won't now either, so move it to the "losers" pile.

Fashion Makeovers. Can the "losers" be restyled to become keepers? Read Fashion Makeovers, page 94, before you toss. Some makeovers are so simple, **anyone** can do them!

Where to Put the "Losers"

1. **Friends or relatives** — Even though it isn't "you," someone else may love it. Barbara's five sisters are her favorite recipients!

2. **Used clothing stores** — You will generally receive 50% of the resale price. Clothes should be clean, pressed, repaired, and seasonally correct. Call ahead since some stores accept clothing only on certain days, or accept items for a specific type of clientele.

3. **Garage sales and swap meets** — Leslie and friends have an annual joint garage sale. (Be careful not to buy each other's losers!)

4. **The Goodwill or Salvation Army** (or other charitable organizations) — the best direction for out-of-season, out-of-style, or irreparable clothing. You can receive a tax deduction equal to the current value of the clothing. Be sure to get a receipt from the agency and keep an accurate list of items donated attached to it. One suggestion — remove special buttons, lace and trims worth saving, since these organizations turn unsold clothing into rags after a certain period of time.

Work With the "Winners"

Snip a swatch of fabric from the seam allowances and staple them to cards cut to fit a wallet photo holder. Put spring/summer on one side, and fall/winter on the other.

This organized swatch collection is your "handbag closet"! You'll be able to quickly see what you need and match future purchases against the swatches. If you love to shop sales, your "handbag closet" can also save you money. A bargain isn't a bargain if you get it home and it doesn't go with anything you already have.

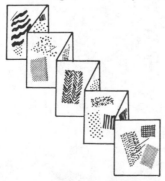

Putting Your Look Together

Do you wonder why everything looks right when someone else puts a look together . . . the right clothes with just the right touch in accessories? Do your fashion homework each season, use these ideas, and YOU CAN become as creative as the fashion pros.

Make An Idea Board

Tape magazine clippings to the inside of your closet door. It will give you ideas of new ways to wear pieces you already own or what to buy to update your wardrobe.

Make a "Scarecrow"

A "scarecrow" is a totally accessorized outfit placed on your bed as if it were on your body. Each season we create new looks from old clothes by scarecrowing. It also helps us to discover missing parts that would make an outfit complete.

While scarecrowing, think of "crossovers" — the things that can do double duty. Think of suits as separates. Can the jacket be teamed with a sweater and pants for casual wear? What new combinations can you visualize? Will a favorite dress work in the office with a jacket and for evening with different accessories? Can your velour warmup suit be used for casual entertaining?

First, cover your bed with a plain sheet if you have a printed bedspread. Put all your "keeper" and "sleeper" skirts, pants, blouses, sweaters, jackets, and dresses on your bed. Then pull out all of your jewelry, belts, scarves, shoes and even fashion hosiery. Leave an empty spot on the bed just your size. No, it's not for napping, but for "scarecrowing". Your bed should look like this:

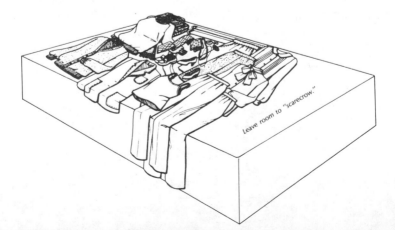

Leave room to "scarecrow."

Create your first scarecrow in the following manner:
- Start with a basic pant or skirt and jacket.
- Add a blouse or sweater.
- Now accessorize it. Be creative — try scarves as belts, group unusual accessory combinations together.
- Now try other bottoms, tops or accessories with the pieces you've arranged on the bed.

Your first scarecrow might be . . .   **Your second scarecrow might be . . .**

Since everything is out in plain sight, new combinations just seem to jump out! You may also discover missing pieces, so make a shopping list. Even "sleepers" may show their worth.

Dress Rehearsal

Scarecrows are great in theory, but you'll never know if the outfits really work for you unless you try them on. It is essential to have a full length mirror. A three-way mirror is even better. It is a real time saver because you can quickly see yourself from all angles.

During the dress rehearsal, ask yourself these questions:
-Does the total look suit you in color, line, and proportion?
-Are you comfortable? Clothes that make you fidget because of fit or appearance will destroy self-confidence.
-Is there something else you need to buy to make it perfect?
-Would changing the length of one of the pieces make it better?
-Would changing to lighter, darker, matching, or textured hosiery make a difference?

Write It Down

When a combination is a winner, write it down. Note additional items you need to buy to make the outfit complete. Adapt the following form to your needs:

Jacket	Skirt or Pant	Blouse	Jewelry	Hosiery	Shoes	Other Accessories

You might also take an instant photo in order to quickly see your new combinations. Tack the list and the photos to your closet door.

How To Look More Interesting

Throughout this book we've given you a very practical approach to wardrobe planning. However, "practical" is sometimes boring. The following ideas can help you develop a flare for the unusual and add interest to your look:

Develop a Trademark

You remember some people for a look that just suits them. The look has become their "trademark." The following are examples of interesting trademarks used by our fashionable friends:

Pam says "Hats make my classic clothes dramatic!"

Tammy has always worn men's ties . . . even when they weren't in fashion.

Mix Textures

Mixing textures is easier than mixing prints and patterns. According to designers Calvin Klein and Bill Blass, it is unexpected texture contrast that adds classic individuality to your look. Follow these guidelines for combining fabric textures:

1. Medium textures are perfect for your wardrobe core because they are the easiest to work with. They combine well with each other and with smooth or bumpy textures. For example, you could put a sweater knit jacket and a satin blouse with your medium textured flannel pants.

2. Extreme textures combine well only if they are similar in both mood and end use. For example, it is . . .

safe — to combine sequins and satin or suede and wool plaids.

unusual — to mix moods and normal end use such as putting sequins on a sweatshirt.

stretching it — to mix fabrics that have a **very strong** mood and end use image. For example, sequins on a lumberjack plaid would end up looking comical. However, if whimsical is your trademark, it could work for you. Really stretching it, however, would be a chiffon ski suit with a terry cloth down vest. These fabrics are not usually used for these items or together.

Mix Prints, Plaids, and Stripes

For print mixing ideas, read European fashion magazines and look at the clothes of Yves St. Laurent, Missoni, Calvin Klein, Perry Ellis, and Koos Van den Akker. Or look at **men**. They mix patterns everyday when they combine suit, tie, and shirt. Read men's fashion magazines. Old patchwork quilts are another source of inspiration.

McCall Patterns' Design Director, Richard Segrin says you will get the best pattern mixes when you tie them together with **either** color **or** design and follow one of these 2 rules:

1. Use **different patterns** that contain the **same or related colors**.
2. Use the **same patterns** in **different colors**. (Limit the mix to 3 or 4 coordinating colors. See page 28 for color mixing ideas.)

The following additional guidelines will help you get started:

1. It is easiest to combine geometrics with other geometrics and florals with florals.

2. When mixing different designs, classics like these menswear patterns are easiest.

glen plaids	pin dots	paisleys or foulard prints	herringbone	pin stripes

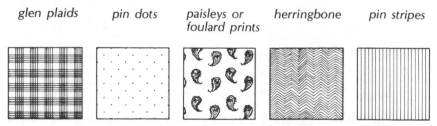

3.   The smaller the patterns, the easier it is to mix them. No two patterns should be the same size.

4.   One pattern should dominate. Texture can be pattern also. Stand 6 feet away to see if texture is creating an obvious pattern.

Don't Ruin Your Image

Attention to detail is the sign of a well-dressed woman. Make sure none of the following are visible to spoil your finished look:

1. Unpolished and/or rundown shoes
2. Hose with reinforced toes in sandal-style shoes
3. Hose with runs
4. Makeup stained or soiled collars
5. Obvious underarm stains
6. Lint or dandruff
7. Missing or hanging buttons, snaps, hooks and eyes
8. Slips that show
9. Slipping lingerie straps
10. Visible bra or panty lines (rear view)
11. Linings that hang below your garment hem
12. Coats too short for the dress or skirt under them
13. Pants and straight skirts that are too tight
14. Blouses that gap at the bustline
15. Clothes that look worn, pilled, frayed, unevenly faded or stained
16. Unkempt hair or old hair style with new looks
17. Unmanicured nails or chipped nail polish

Determine Your Needs

Categorize Your Clothes

Remember that the activities in your life should dictate the types of clothing you have. Refer to your lifestyle and wardrobe pies (pages 17 & 18) and group your clothes into appropriate categories. Do you have too many or not enough clothes in any category?

Working Wardrobes — A Special Consideration

Clothes alone don't get you ahead, but if you want to be a success in your field, you must look successful. Observe the people you work with and consider your work environment and any dress codes before planning wardrobe additions. If you meet and work with new people constantly, you can manage with fewer and better pieces.

Work environments can be broken down into 3 types with typical clothing for each:

Business Attitude	Business Type	Image	Clothes
Conservative	Banking & finance, law, personnel	Reliable, intelligent, competent	Conservative matched suits and classic dress styles in quiet darker colors
Public Oriented and Service	Insurance, real estate, teaching, sales	Authoritative, knowledgable, trustworthy, warm	More casual variations of conservative looks: unmatched suits, sweater jackets, tailored trousers
Trend Setting	Advertising, fashion, arts, show business	Up-to-date, literate, creative	Trend-setting styles more acceptable, anything goes in some fields.

Put Your Needs in Writing

After analyzing your wardrobe, list the items you need. Be specific! "Pants" is not enough to help you avoid impulse purchases. Write down color, style, fabric type, and the pieces you intend to wear with it. For example:

I need

Black wool gabardine trousers
Red silk blouse
To go with black and white tweed blazer.

Black walking shoes
To go with grey or black pants
Black and white argyle knee high stockings
to wear with black shoes

Budget Your Time and Money

Decide which of your needs you should sew, which you should buy, and which could be fashion makeovers.

Balance Your Wardrobe Budget

To decide how much money you can afford to spend on new clothes, look at your check stubs and receipts for the last year. How much did you spend on clothing, accessories and fabric? Use this figure as a guide in planning your current budget.

The largest slice of your clothing budget should be spent on the largest slice of your wardrobe pie (see page 18). However, we might spend more for an item that won't get lots of wear because we feel that our impression at a certain event is important. Calculating a cost per wearing will certainly bring you back to reality before you spend a lot of money or sewing time on that item.

Figure the Cost Per Wearing

When deciding if a wardrobe addition is a good investment for you, consider its cost per wearing, not just the initial cost. $200 may seem like a lot to pay for a winter coat until you discover the cost per wearing would only be 80¢ . . . not so bad after all!

Cost per wearing formula:

COST	÷	NUMBER OF WEARINGS	=	COST PER WEARING
$200 + $50	÷	312	=	80¢
(Cost of coat)	(Cleaning + for 2 years)	(6 wearings per week × 26 weeks × 2 years)		

When to Sew and When to Buy

Practice the rule of three whether you sew or buy: if an item goes with at least 3 things already in your closet and can be worn to at least 3 different events, it is a good investment. Everything you want doesn't have to meet this criteria, but it can help you weed out poor investments.

We believe the best wardrobes are a combination of things you make (or have a dressmaker sew) and things you buy. At times it doesn't make sense to sew. Learn to develop a healthy balance rather than face an empty closet or a bad case of the "sewer's guilties"!

It Makes Sense to Sew

1.   When you can't find what you want in ready-to-wear.
2.   When you can make something in less time than it would take to shop for it.
3.   When you're capable of turning out better quality clothing in better fabric than you can afford ready-made.
4.   When you are feeling guilty about the size of your fabric stash!
5.   When you find expensive accessories that would be simple to copy. We've copied a $26 silk necktie in 20 minutes for 1/8th the price. (We share instructions for this neat tie on page 67).

It Makes More Sense to Buy

1.   When your time and effort are worth more than the money saved if you made it. We value our sewing time — you should too!
2.   When you don't have the time to make what you need.
3.   When the details or fabric are beyond your sewing skills.
4.   When you want to treat yourself because you've earned it by sewing just about everything else you wear!
5.   When the color, fit, and design lines are perfect for you and so is the price tag.
6.   When you find a great item in a great fabric at a great price . . . even if it needs minor adjustments in detail or fit. Barbara bought two skirts in the wrong size because the fabrics were unique and the skirts were true bargains. It took less than an hour to restyle and refit . . . well worth the effort.

> NOTE: These are ready-to-wear adjustments that should be fast and simple enough for you or your dressmaker to do:
>
> - Replace average looking buttons with distinctive ones.
> - Add a fashionable belt.
> - Redo poorly done hems (see page 96).
> - Change length for better proportion (see page 96).
> - Add trim or replace inferior trims.
> - Add or remove shoulder pads for a smoother fit (see page 101).
> - Lower too-tight armholes (see page 100).
> - Taper side seams for closer-to-the-body fit (see page 100).

Don't Buy or Sew

1.   When a fashion is soon to disappear. (See Chapter 2).
2.   If it won't work with at least one other thing in your closet.
3.   Just because it is on sale. If you love sales, but feel impulse will rule reason, shop a day or two before a sale starts and examine store merchandise at your leisure. Make a list of items that are your color and on your list of wardrobe needs. Reason will then be more likely to prevail over the emotional excitement the day of the sale.

Be a Savvy Shopper

Develop Store Savvy

The best clothing investments whether you sew or buy . . .

- Will be classic styles that survive the whims of fashion.
- Can be worn year round because of color and fabric.
- Will hold shape due to quality fabric and construction.
- Will suit your style.
- Will work with something already in your closet.

Seasonless Dressing

Think of your next wardrobe purchase in terms of year round dressing. Donna Karan, designer for Anne Klein believes at least 30% of a woman's wardrobe should be in seasonless fabrics and colors.

Think of fabrics by color and weight, not by fiber content. Wool is thought of as a winter fabric, but lightweight tan wool gabardine pants could be worn almost year round, as can dark cottons. These seasonless colors and fabrics make great investments:

Seasonless Colors	Seasonless Fabrics
navy	lightweight wool gabardine and flannel
black	wool crepe, georgette, voile, and gauze
beige	wool or rayon challis
white	wool or silk jersey knits
red	silk or linen suitings
purple	silk and silky synthetic blouse weight
olive	fabrics (open weaves will be cooler in
cream	hot weather)
medium and light grey	cotton knits and velour
periwinkle blue	Ultrasuede® brand fabric and other synthetic
camel	suedes
cocoa	corduroy (pinwale and feathercord)
tan	denim
taupe	rayon crepe and all crepe de chines.

Quality Checks

Try on the most expensive garments you can find. Quality is generally reflected in the cost of a garment, but designers' names influence pricing and are not always an assurance of quality. Buy the best quality you can afford. It's false economy to buy lower quality than you can afford; replacements almost always cost more the next year due to inflation.

Quality Check Chart — Look for These Details:

GOOD	NOT SO GOOD

Seams:
5/8" seam allowances and 10-12 stitches per inch.

Seams pucker, seam allowances too narrow for altering.

Edges and corners:
Flat and without bulk.

Notches and corners pucker.

Zippers:
Thread should match, stitching should be straight and without puckers.

Teeth show, stitching uneven, puckered.

Stripes and plaids:
Should match at all major seams.

Mismatched or uneven at hemline.

Topstitching:
Thread should match fabric (unless done for contrast), stitches should be even and without puckers.

Stitching that is crooked.

Hems:
Should be invisible from right side.

Hem edge forms a ridge on the outside. Stitching is tight so hem puckers.

Buttonholes:
Should be even and without loose threads.

Stitching is spaced too far apart to prevent raveling.

Buttons:
Should be attached securely and have thread shank if fabric is bulky.

Loose threads.

Sanity Saving Shopping Tips

1. Shop in season. It might cost more, but it saves you time if merchandise is current and plentiful for best selection.
2. Shop when stores are least crowded, usually weekday mornings before 11:30 am or at dinnertime — 5 to 7 pm.
3. Shop in bad weather when everyone else stays home.
4. Get to know the layout of your favorite store. Our friend, Roz, is a shopping wizard who can "case" a store in minutes making lunch hour shopping a snap.
5. Call to be sure that what you saw in an ad is still available.
6. Don't wait until the last minute to shop, you'll buy something out of frustration that you won't like later.
7. Shop at home with mail order catalogues.
8. Find **your** kind of store and stick with it. Small stores or boutiques might offer you more personal attention, but a department store offers one-stop shopping. Find a salesperson in your favorite store or department who knows your taste and who will keep you informed of new arrivals and special sales.
9. Shop better ready-to-wear. Designers and better manufacturers design their lines around coordinates to help you save time putting pieces together.
10. If you don't have time or you **hate** to shop, join the "H-I-D" ("have-it-done") club! Better department and specialty stores offer personal shopping services to save you time and frustration. Make your list and hand it over (or even phone it in)! They do the footwork and put everything into a fitting room. All you do is try on and make your selections. Painless shopping — and at no extra charge!
11. ALWAYS ALWAYS ALWAYS shop with your all important "hand-bag closet" and color swatches so that even impulse purchases will work in your wardrobe. (See pages 71 and 25.)

Dollar Saving Ideas

1. **Snoop shop first** with your list of needs to see where you will get the most for your money. Purchase later.
2. **Look for department crossovers**. Sometimes you can find evening clothes in loungewear and sundresses in swimwear for less money.
3. **Shop the boy's department**. Designer label sportswear is 25% to 50% less in boy's wear than in women's wear. Use the size conversion chart below for shirts, sweaters and jackets.

Misses/Junior size	Boy's size
5-6	14
7-8	16
9-10	18
11-12	20

If you are slim in the hips, try both boy's and menswear departments for pants which are sized by waist and length. You can save at least $10 on casual pants and alterations are usually free!

4. **Take advantage of sales.** It pays to plan wardrobe needs and snoop shop early in the season. Three to four weeks later go back for markdowns that can save you 10-20%. Become familiar with a store's sale schedule so you can plan major purchases with savings in mind. As a charge customer, you'll get advance notification of sales. Record these and other advertised store sale dates for the future. Hosiery and lingerie are generally marked down only twice a year when the manufacturers have special sales. Stock up then!

5. **Go to a sale prepared.** Do your homework first and shop the departments that interest you right after you receive notice of the event. Sales people will often let you know what's going to be marked down. Sometimes you can shop the night before a sale and pay the sale price. "Special purchase" can indicate items brought in only for the sale, and can be a real bargain. Often, they are manufacturer's closeouts or discontinued designs.

Discount Clothing Stores and Factory Outlets

These stores are popping up all over the country. They keep their prices low because customer services are kept to a minimum. To make the most of shopping these stores:

1. Shop often since their selection is hit or miss, feast or famine. Don't lock yourself into the idea that you **have to buy** each time you run in to check the racks.

2. Be prepared for communal dressing rooms. Modesty is difficult. Dress comfortably, in easy-to-remove clothing.

3. Take cash because many do not accept credit cards and store charge accounts at these stores are uncommon.

4. Make purchase decisions carefully. Many stores have a strict, no-return no-exchange policy.

5. Discount stores that carry designer clothing usually cut the labels out but the designer is indicated on the fiber content tag by a number preceded by "RN" (Registered Number) or "WPL" (Wool Products Labeling). If you're label conscious, you can consult the RN and WPL Directory from the Federal Trade Commission in the reference room at your library for your favorite designer's numbers.

6. You'll find a mix of quality in discount clothing and factory outlet stores because they stock the following:
- **discontinued designs and manufacturer's overruns** (more goods were produced than sold to regular retailers)
- **cancelled retail orders or overstocks**

• **seconds** (items that didn't pass first quality inspection) Flaws and imperfections are often difficult to detect or if they are visible, you might have the sewing skills to repair the problem.

• **damaged merchandise** Check carefully to be sure you can repair or camouflage the damage; otherwise, don't waste your money.

• **incorrectly sized merchandise** Don't trust the tag. Try on more than one size and assume that two pieces labeled as the same size, aren't.

• **one-of-a-kind designer samples** (merchandise sold to discounters at the end of the manufacturer's selling season) Sample sizes are usually 6, 8 or 10 and 16 or 18 in large size fashions.

Resale Shops Can Be Great!

Find the ones that are selective and carry superior quality, little worn things rather than things that already look worn. This type of shop is often sponsored by fund raising women's groups or charitable organizations. Those located in affluent suburbs usually have the most fashionable selections. One woman's trash is another woman's treasure!

6 Steps to Simplify Fabric Shopping

1. Select a bottom weight fabric (one you would make into a skirt, pant and jacket) in a color you would like.
2. Carry that one bolt of fabric around the store to see how many things you can find to go with it. Select top weights for blouses and two-piece dresses.
3. If nothing goes with it, don't buy it. You're not likely to find anything at any other store either!
4. If you did find a lot of top weights that coordinate, do they include any prints that introduce a second and third color? This gives you an opportunity to find another bottom weight that would work with the group.
5. Place all possible choices on a table and by mixing and matching, narrow your selection to what you need. Check your selections against your "handbag closet" (see page 71) to see how the new pieces will work with what you already own.
6. Don't feel you have to sew all the pieces at once, but buying all of the coordinates at one time protects you against seasonal color change in fashion.

Make the Best Marriage of Pattern and Fabric

Successfully combining pattern and fabric is the most creative part of sewing. It can also be the most difficult. Experienced fashion designers can look at or feel a piece of fabric and visualize it as a finished garment. The only real difference between you and them might be time and practice. Have you ever wondered whether it's easier to start with the pattern or the fabric? Designers do both.

Starting With Fabric

Like true "fabric-aholics", when we enter a fabric store, we rarely make a beeline to the pattern department. There is just too much to see along the way! If most of your projects start with the fabric too, consider the following guidelines as you make your pattern choices.

1.   If you're choosing a pattern for a print, plaid, or stripe, make sure there are no restrictions for these fabrics on the back of the pattern envelope.

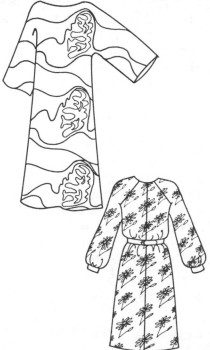

   -Almost any pattern design is suitable for small to medium scale all-over prints.
   -Prints with large design motifs require more fabric. Use the "with nap" yardage. Also, choose simple styles as the details would just get lost in the fabric. Let the fabric tell you how to style it. Leslie stood back and just looked at her wonderful Hawaiian screen print and decided to make it into a simple caftan with kimono sleeves in order to make the most of the design.
   -Prints with obvious motifs or one way designs look better when they match at major seamlines.

2. Simple fabrics with less surface design or texture can take details and more seaming. Construction details don't get lost in flannel, gabardine, broadcloth, jersey, crepe de chine, and silk and linen suitings.

3. Crisp fabrics are suitable for tailored silhouettes. Without darts and seams to shape them to body contours, they can make you look boxy and geometric.

4. Soft, fluid, lightweight fabrics are best in softer designs with little detail. Applied pieces like band collars and pockets are bound to droop. (See **Sensational Silk** for all silky fabric how-to's. See page 128.)

5. Sheer fabrics require simple designs, fewer seams, and limited details. Unless you underline a sheer fabric, inside pockets, facings, and zippers would show through to the outside. (See **Sew A Beautiful Wedding** for tips for sewing on sheers. See page 128.)

6. The softer and more drapeable the fabric, the more gathers you can use without getting a bulky look. Gathers work in chiffon, but would be bulky in a sweater knit.

7. Pile fabrics like velvet, velveteen, corduroy, and velours are easiest to sew when seams and added detail are kept to a minimum. The major problem in sewing these fabrics is seam slippage and seam puckering.

8. Choose a pattern with simple lines and fewer details for any fabric beyond your current level of sewing skill. Trying new fabrics will expand your fabric and sewing knowhow.

9. Border prints, panel or scarf prints and bordered eyelets can limit pattern choice, but a little creative thinking will help you use these designs in new ways.

Cut both blouse fronts on the border as a mirror image. Use button and loop closures. Repeat on center front seam on skirt.

Think of a border as a ribbon and miter it around an armhole for an unusual detail.

Asymetric vertical placement of a border is a good lengthening line.

Careful placement of a border print can make a simple vest exciting.

Place an eyelet border at the bottom edges.

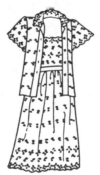

Two matching 34" scarf squares make a soft dirndl for most figures. Use a third for a shawl.

Starting With the Pattern

When you have an itemized list of wardrobe needs, you might find it easier to choose the pattern first. You can look for specific styling and details and then look for the right fabric. Choosing the pattern first gives you more freedom in style choice because you don't have to deal with the limitations of a fabric you have already purchased. The following steps will help you find the right fabric for your pattern:

1. If you aren't inspired by the illustration or photo on the pattern, go snoop shopping for fabric and color ideas in similar styles. Look at photos in other pattern catalogues too.

2.	If you are limited in fabric choice because some or all of the suggested fabrics are not available, improvise just as you would in the kitchen when you don't have all the right ingredients. Look for other fabrics that have a similar feel and drape as those listed.

3.	If a pattern is suitable for both soft and crisp fabrics, those listed are usually similar in weight but they will hang differently.

4.	To see how a fabric will look, drape it on your body to simulate the design. If the design has gathers, gather the fabric in your hands. Do the gathers fall softly or stand away from your body? Would the fabric drape better on the bias?

How to Shop the Pattern Catalogue

1.	Scan **all** pattern brands to see trends. Make a list of patterns you like and similar designs in different catalogues (note prices).

2.	There are 650 to 700 designs in each catalogue. If your time is limited, read only the front editorial pages and the front of each tabbed section. Pattern companies spend thousands of dollars on these pages to show you wardrobe coordinating ideas, new fashion colors and fabric combinations, and featured accessories.

3.	Pattern companies are fashion right. They see the same shows as ready-to-wear buyers 6 months in advance of the season so they have time to put the same designs in their catalogues. They also give you time to plan ahead by sending catalogues to the stores 2 months in advance of the cover date. For example, the March-dated catalogues will arrive in the stores in January.

4.	40 to 50 new designs are added each month. A major discard of slow selling patterns takes place every three months. When a pattern has a shared billing with another on the same page, it may be on its way out. If it's a pattern you like, buy it now. However, recently pattern companies have been moving out of season patterns to the back of the section and doubling them up on a page. For example, a classic coat won't get top billing in the summer.

5.	Look at all sections regardless of their captions. Barbara made a velour robe from an evening dress pattern.

6.	Patterns labeled "easy" generally contain fewer pieces and simplified instructions. Any patterns with these details can be fast:
- gathers rather than darts or pleats
- few details, like plackets or yokes
- simple neckline finishes (a facing instead of a collar)
- no pieces cut on the bias

7. The line drawings show design details and seamlines. The photos of the fashion show fabric and accessories.

8. Suggested fabrics are those considered most suitable for the design. The garment has been made by pattern company dressmakers in the proper weight fabric to test drape. When it says "not suitable for . . .", it means it won't work or won't give you a quality look. Every pattern is made up half in muslin and half in gingham or plaid. If the plaid cannot be matched at the major center fronts and backs and side seams, then these fabrics are considered unsuitable.

There's Tons of Information on Pattern Envelope

1. **The envelope front** shows the various views you can choose.

2. **Backviews** show the true shape of the design and its details.

3. **Yardage requirements** are very accurate today because trial layouts are done by computer. (Don't buy less unless you're short.)

4. **Yardage block** lists fabric widths best suited to the pattern design and pieces. If your fabric width is not listed, check the back of most pattern catalogues for a "fabric conversion chart," or do a trial layout. Finished garment widths at lower edges help you judge ease at the bottom edge — a clue to pattern adjustments needed before cutting. The finished lengths can be compared to jacket, skirt, and pant lengths you've found flattering.

5. **Garment description** elaborates on fit and details that might not be obvious in pictures such as "dropped shoulders" or "blousoned". Most patterns are made to body measurements plus **standard wearing ease** (room to wiggle or to have lunch), and have **design ease** which creates fashion. Here's how a jacket would look with these fit descriptions:

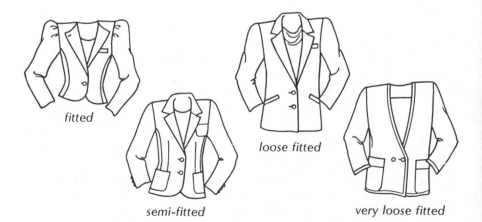

fitted

loose fitted

semi-fitted

very loose fitted

Pattern companies tell us they allow the following amounts of ease in the bust and hips of various types of garments with these fit descriptions:

| Silhouette | Total Ease in Bust Area | | | Total Ease in |
	Dresses, Shirts Tops, Vests, (bust area)	Lined or Unlined Jackets (bust area)	Lined or Unlined Coats	Pants, Skirts Culottes
Close Fitting	0-1½"	—	—	—
Fitted	3"	3"-3⅞"	3⅞"-5⅛"	2"
Semi-fitted	3⅛"-4½"	4"-6"	5¼"-8"	2⅛"-3"
Loosely Fitted	4⅝"-8"	6⅛"-10"	8⅛"-12"	3⅛"-6"
Very Loosely Fitted	Over 8"	Over 10"	Over 12"	Over 6"

Make the Best Marriage of Pattern and Fabric

If you can answer "yes" to all or most of these questions, you have planned a wardrobe winner! If not, reconsider or make some changes in the planned purchase.

Yes   No

_____ _____ Does this project satisfy a need in my wardrobe plan? Impulse purchases often end up never sewn or half finished.

_____ _____ If I can't make it up right away, is it a seasonless fabric that won't go out of fashion before I sew it?

_____ _____ Is the color right for me and will it work with three things I already have in my wardrobe?

_____ _____ If I've worn this fiber before, was it comfortable?

_____ _____ Am I willing to care for this fabric as the manufacturer recommends?

_____ _____ Are the design and texture of the fabric flattering to me? (Hold the fabric up to you in front of a mirror and stand 3 feet away to evaluate.)

_____ _____ Do the design lines in the pattern enhance my figure assets and minimize my figure problems?

_____ _____ Are the construction details of the pattern and fabric within my sewing abilities?

_____ _____ Have I tried on or made a similar style before? Was it comfortable and flattering?

_____ _____ Is it on the up side of the fashion curve so I will get enough wear out of it to merit the time and money I am planning to spend?

_____ _____ Does the total cost plus the time required to sew fit my time/money budget? (Be sure to consider the cost of maintenance.)

Be Your Own Designer

You can individualize patterns if you just know how to change a few details. Don't be afraid to repeat something you love. Ready-to-wear designers often repeat successful silhouettes, details, even favorite fabrics from season to season.

There are many other reasons for using patterns more than once:

1. You can eliminate most pattern fitting adjustments after the first time.

2. Making a pattern the second time is faster than the first.

3. If your fabric is expensive or one you haven't sewn before, there is security in using a familiar pattern.

4. Different moods or seasons can be expressed by sewing the same pattern in different fabrics. For example, use the same cardigan, camisole and soft skirt patterns in different fabrics to create these looks.

- Use velvet to create an evening suit look and satin for the camisole.

- Use linen for the jacket and a cotton print for skirt and camisole for a sundress look

Personalize a pattern to look different every time you sew it.

Jacket Ideas

Round the lapel and collar edges on a blazer. Use a French curve to get an accurate curve.

Eliminate vents in blazer sleeves and center back to speed up sewing and create a dressier look.

Topstitch ribbon onto a jacket collar before sewing collar onto jacket.

Blouse Ideas

Change button placement — use sets of two in place of single buttons.

Add a ruffle to a collar band instead of the collar.

Pinch bottom of hemmed straight (not fitted) sleeve and sew buttonhole through both layers. Lap and button.

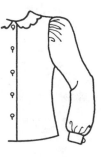

Combine Pattern Pieces

You can combine pieces from several patterns to create new designs as long as they are the same size. Some things are easier to interchange than others. It's fairly simple to exchange tops and bottoms in dresses with waist seams, to switch cuffs and pockets, and to change collar shapes.

Sleeves are easiest to interchange when you use two patterns of the same brand. It's also easier to interchange two shirt sleeves, or two normal set-in sleeves.

Blouse A has a normal fitted set-in sleeve. Blouse B is fuller and has narrower shoulders (which prevents you from having football player shoulders).

Always do a tissue overlay of the two bodices to check the curve and size of the armhole and the length and slope of the shoulder.

This is the result of the two combined. The armhole of A was recut so sleeve B would fit.

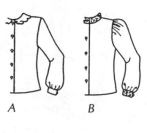

A   B

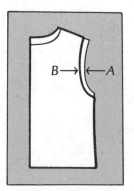

B→ ←A

Fashion Makeovers

Don't be reluctant to remodel a garment just because it was expensive or it took hours to sew. Better to refit, restyle, or recycle than to let it hang in the closet and become a museum piece. You can make changes that put "sleepers" back into circulation by updating them. To decide if something is worth the energy to make over, ask yourself:

- How much time will it take?
- Is the fabric worth the time and effort?
- Would it be easier or less expensive to make or buy a replacement?
- Are the seam allowances deep enough to allow letting out?
- Will topstitching, pockets, or other details get in the way of altering?
- Will original stitching or hem lines show?
- If you plan to use scraps left over from sewing the garment, do they still match?

We will concentrate on making over the old, but the techniques and ideas apply to new clothes as well. Some ready-made garments need minor changes to fit or look better, and you can save a fortune by doing them yourself!

The Simplest Makeover — Wear It a New Way!

Wear a shirtdress as a long jacket.

Wear a shirt as a jacket or beach coverup.

Crisscross the points of a too-wide collar and hold in place with a pretty pin.

Wear a worn shirt under a crew neck sweater. If collar is the wrong size, tuck points in.

Makeovers That Require Sewing — Do You Have the Best Tools?

New Items

Grabbit — a wonderful magnetic pin catcher with a wide, shallow surface that holds lots of pins. Turn it upside down to pick up spilled pins!

Pinch and pull type bodkin — great for replacing elastic — the tweezer end grabs elastic, ring locks it in place.

Snag-Nab-It™ — repairs snags in knitted and woven fabrics.

Fray Check™ — a liquid ravel preventer. Run a thin stream along the edge of a seam for a permanent seam finish. Use to stop runs in pantyhose too!

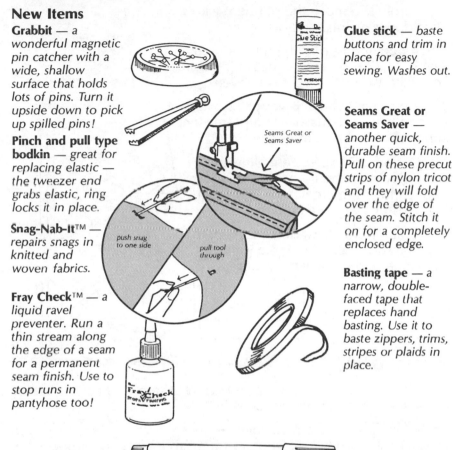

Glue stick — baste buttons and trim in place for easy sewing. Washes out.

Seams Great or Seams Saver — another quick, durable seam finish. Pull on these precut strips of nylon tricot and they will fold over the edge of the seam. Stitch it on for a completely enclosed edge.

Basting tape — a narrow, double-faced tape that replaces hand basting. Use it to baste zippers, trims, stripes or plaids in place.

Erasable markers — great for marking hems and button placement. Just touch with a damp cloth to erase. There are 3 kinds.

- Water erasable with dark ink: Mark-B-Gone, Wonder Marker
- Water erasable for marking dark colored fabrics: Nonce Marking Pencil
- Air erasable (disappears in 24-48 hours without water — no procrastinating!): Dritz Disappearing Ink Pen or the Vanishing Marker.

The Basic Necessities:

1. **Sharp** 8" dressmaker shears
2. **Sharp** embroidery scissors
3. Hand needles — size 10 sharps for hemming
4. Measuring tools — tape measure, yardstick, sewing gauge
5. Seam ripper
6. Skirt-pant hooks — both black and silver for light and dark fabrics

Shorten or Lengthen with a Perfect Hem

1. Carefully remove the old hem with a seam ripper or small scissors.

2. Try on and turn up hem to desired length. Mark new length, measuring from floor with yardstick if skirt is uneven.

new hem length ↓

3. Press hem lightly. Never press over top edge of hem — it may leave a permanent impression on the right side.

4. Cut off any excess hem allowance. Hem allowance should be 1½" to 2" for most garments, narrower for lightweight full skirts or bias cut garments.

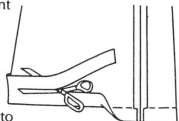

5. Grade seam allowances inside hem to ¼". Ease stitch edge of hem and finish using one of the following if necessary.

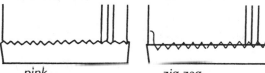

| pink
(most invisible) | zig-zag
(more durable) | attach seam binding
(more finished looking) |

6. Now hem with the perfect hem stitch, **the blind hem**, which will never leave a ridge on the outside.

   • Use size 10 sharp needles — these finer needles allow you to catch only a fiber of your outside fabric so hemming stitches won't show.
   • Use polyester thread (single strand) — it's the strongest thread so hems will last.
   • Fold down hem edge and hem between the two layers. Use long loose running stitches at least ½" apart. Catch only a fiber of the outside fabric. Every 6" pull on the stitches to loosen them and knot in hem allowance for security.

Shorten the Easy Way

Use tucks. They are perfect for border prints since it won't disturb the border, and for straight or dirndl skirts. Don't use on A-line or bias skirts.

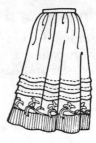

On Sleeves and Hem Lines

Two tucks or more create the best proportion:

1. Mark tuck stitching lines with washable marker. Space evenly using a sewing gauge or ruler.

2. Pin or baste in place.

3. Try on to make sure spacing and proportion are pleasing.

4. Stitch, press.

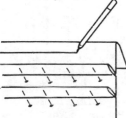
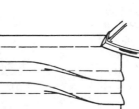

Shorten From the Top

This works well when you need a bit more waistline room and want to shorten a garment, too. Use this on border prints and eyelets because it doesn't disturb the bottom edge, also on A-lines. Use caution with side slant trouser pockets. More than 1" will shorten the pocket too much.

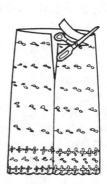

1. Remove waistband and zipper.

2. Cut excess length off of top, leaving a ⅝" seam allowance.

3. Lengthen any darts or change them into soft gathers.

4. Replace zipper and waistband.

Lengthening and Other Tricks

Remove the old hem and press crease out. Pin new length and hem as on page 96. For a stubborn hem crease, try a mixture of half white vinegar and half water on your press cloth — the vinegar helps to unset the old crease. If the crease still shows, stitch trim along the line or several rows of topstitching to camouflage it.

If letting the hem down is undesirable:

Add a flounce in matching or contrasting color

Add a contrast band of stripe or a plaid cut on the bias

Use sleeves for a pieced waist-band. Gather waist.

Make sure it's long enough to tuck in or wear as overblouse.

Turn a high waisted dress into a skirt.

Turn a dress into a shirt

When Pant Lengths Change

Cut off 1½" to 2" below knee for knickers. Use cut off leg fabric for bands. If wearing with boots, make sure they will meet boot top.

Cut off at hem fold and add purchased ribbing for cuffs. Works for knickers, too.

Pants full enough through knee area make great bermuda shorts.

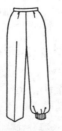

Fashion Updates

Tapering pants: Remove hem. Pin inseam and outseam deeper equally at the hem, tapering to knee on the inseam and to the full hip on the outseam. Try on to test new width. Stitch. Hem.

Tapering A-line skirts: Pin side seams deeper as shown. Try on to test. Stitch. Hem.

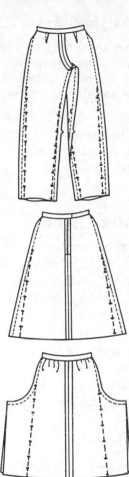

Turn a culotte into a skirt: Remove inseam stitching and restitch center front and center back straight down from just above crotch curve. Trim seam to ⅝", press open.

Quick party looks: These changes are temporary.

-Hand baste satin ribbon over outseams for a tuxedo pant look.

-Hand baste an inverted pleat in bottom of pant leg for a dressy, skinny pant look.

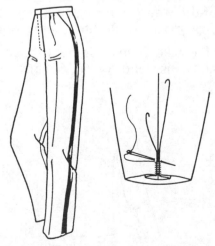

Narrow a Shoulder — 2 Methods

1. Gather shoulders on both sides of shoulder seamline. Secure by stitching gathered area to seam tape on inside.

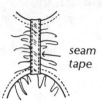

seam tape

2. Make 2 or 3 tucks at shoulder line on front and back. Pin in first to check placement. Stitch.

Make More Room

When an armhole is too snug, stitch underarm seam ¼″ lower through sleeve and garment. Trim seam allowance to ¼″. Repeat if even more room is needed.

If a pant or jumpsuit is too short in the crotch, the same principle as the armhole applies. Stitch crotch lower by ¼″ as shown, trim to ¼″. Repeat if necessary.

Save a Jacket

Worn elbows in classic jackets can be covered with pre-cut leather patches available at your fabric store. Or, use Ultrasuede® brand fabric cut to shape. Remove lining sleeve hem and push lining out of the way. Center patch over elbow. Try on to check. Stitch by hand or machine. Restitch lining hem.

If a jacket style is too boxy for your shape, taper in side seams at waist. Pin first and try on. Stitch.

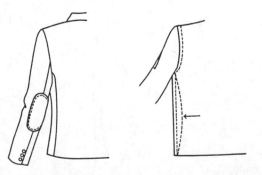

For Better Shoulder Fit

Add shoulder pads if you have these wrinkles:

Remove shoulder pads or use thinner ones if you have these wrinkles:

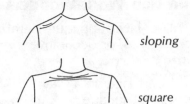

sloping

square

To position shoulder pad, try on garment and adjust pad to proper position.

Pin pad in place from outside, extending it ¼" - ½" into sleeve cap.

On inside, tack pads to shoulder and armhole seam allowances.

Remedies for Outdated or Frayed Shirt Collars and Cuffs

• Remove stitching at top of collar band. Pull out and discard collar.

Restitch top edge of band.

Or, add lace or eyelet between the layers before restitching.

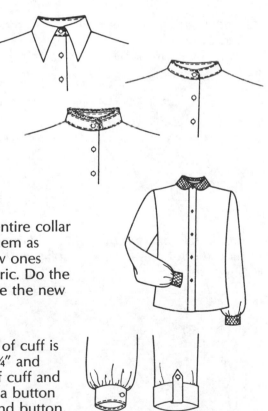

• Remove the entire collar and/or band. Use them as patterns and cut new ones from contrasting fabric. Do the same with cuffs to tie the new color in.

• If lower edge of cuff is frayed, turn under ¼" and topstitch. Or, cut off cuff and hem bottom. Make a button tab, roll up sleeve and button.

Trim Can Work Wonders

Use lace, appliques, embroidery, ribbon, Ultrasuede® brand fabric scraps, or decorative trim to camouflage moth holes, cigarette burns or stains.

Insert lace on a silky blouse — use glue stick to hold in place. Stitch around all edges with a tiny zig-zag. Cut away fabric underneath if desired.

Appliques can cover snags or stains. Repeat on cuffs for design unity.

Lace hanky points can be appliqued to blouse front, collar, or cuffs by hand or by machine.

Camouflage a stained neckline and cuff edges with bias binding.

A pretty floral applique or trim can hide moth holes or stains in a sweater.

Hide worn edges of jacket collar and lapels with bias binding. Repeat on sleeve hem edges.

Get Yourself Organized

You should be able to see everything every time you open the closet door so you can see your range of outfit possibilities. Notions departments, hardware and office supply stores, mail order catalogues, and closet shops are great sources for storage and organization help.

1. **Hang everything you can.** Don't put anything in drawers that you can hang or stack on open shelves.

2. Double your hanging space by creating two hanging levels so you can see tops in relation to bottoms. You'll be amazed at how many new combinations suddenly appear! Buy a system or make your own — use screw eyes, S-hooks, chain, and a dowel for a super easy system:

 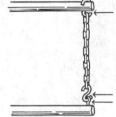

3. **Create functional doors.** Use the inside of doors for extra hanging space. Add towel bars for sweaters or scarves, mug racks for jewelry, nails for belts, or shoe racks.

4. **See-through plastic boxes** are great for dust-free shelf storage. Look for easier to use slide-out drawers, rather than lift-off lids.

5. **Make your closet light and bright.** To avoid investing in professional wiring, buy a battery-operated light from the hardware store. Or, use a clamp-on spotlight directed toward your closet. Give your closet a real lift with a fresh coat of light-colored paint or wallpaper.

A Well-Organized Closet Can Help You Get Dressed

Hang your clothes in categories according to color for easy coordination:

jackets	skirts	evening clothes
blouses	dresses	sleepwear (robes and gowns)
pants	active sportswear	outerwear (jackets, coats, raincoats)

Hang two-piece dresses and suits separately. This will maximize the wearing of each top and bottom. Hang pants, skirts, and dresses close to blouses and jackets so you can easily see ways to mix and maximize — blouses under dresses or jackets over dresses.

The Ideal Closet

Most of us would have to remodel to get our own "ideal" closet. Leslie's closet space was so limited, she consulted with a professional and had her closet redesigned with double hanging rods and adjustable shelves. Because she anticipated moving, she had it installed against two boards inserted at each closet end in order to take the whole system with her. It will need only minor adjustments to be installed in a new home.

The following closet should give you some ideas. Pick what you can use with your existing space or if you're ready — remodel!

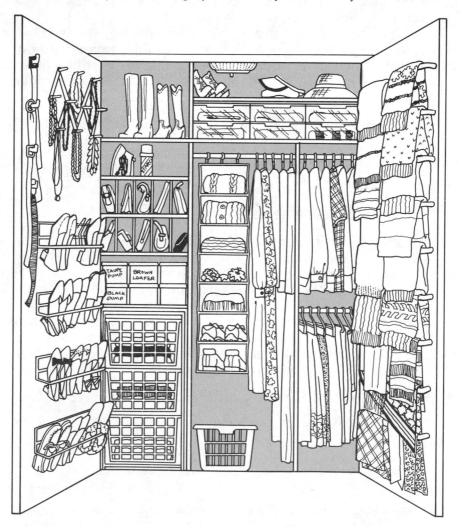

Storage Specifics:

Belts:

1. Hooks placed along side closet wall or back of closet door

2. Men's tie rack mounted on wall or back of closet door

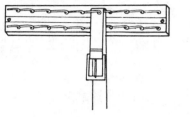

3. Cup hooks screwed into bottom of large wooden hanger

Scarves:

1. Press and clip to skirt hanger or man's pants hanger

2. Clip to clothes pins attached to a wire hanger. Hang on wall for a splash of color!

Jewelry:

1. Closet hooks

2. Mug rack

3. Silverware organizer

Hosiery:

1. Use plastic zip-lock bags to store by color and style (toes, sandalfoot, knee-hi's). Label with self-adhesive stickers and organize in a drawer. Store out of season hose and tights this way in bottom of out-of-season garment bags.

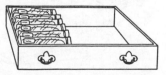

2. Don't toss hose with runs. Save them to wear with boots or under pants. Tie a knot in them so you can find them without trying on!

Handbags

1. Build in vertical dividers on closet shelves.

2. Use see-through wire baskets, on shelves or free-standing.

3. Buy see-through handbag or sweater caddies to store bags, hats, scarves.

Shoes and Boots

1. Shoe caddies come in all sizes to mount on closet doors, hang from the closet rod, or stand on the floor.

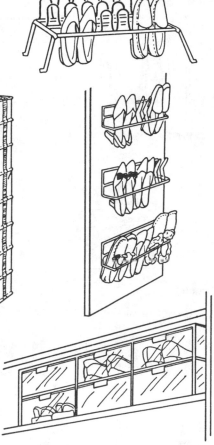

2. See-through plastic boxes are great for shelf storage.

3. If you use ordinary shoe boxes for shoe storage, label the outside end with color and style. We both store ours this way, organizing them by color and rotating the stacks each season.

4. Boot trees prevent cracking that occurs when boot tops fold over. You can make your own by rolling stiff cardboard into tubes to tuck inside boots.

5. Keep your shoes fresh with sweet smelling toe shapes. Check the pattern catalogues for a pattern. Stuff with polyester fiberfill soaked in your favorite perfume.

8 Storage Tips For Getting Longer Life Out of Your Clothes

1. Toss all wire hangers — they leave shoulder creases and provide little support. Take your "empties" back to the dry cleaner for recycling and use some of these instead:

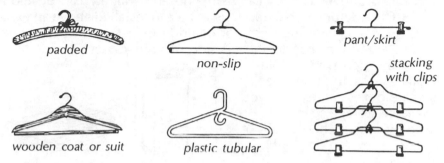

padded

non-slip

pant/skirt

stacking with clips

wooden coat or suit

plastic tubular

2. Don't crowd your clothes. Let them hang freely to prevent closet wrinkles.
3. Fold stretchy bias garments and stretchy knit dresses.
4. Prevent shoulder distortion in better dresses by adding long loops of seam tape anchored to front and back waistline seam. Loops should be slightly shorter than waist to shoulder length to prevent stretch.

5. Keep fragile items like lace, beads, velvet and suede in cloth garment bags for protection. If beaded things are really heavy, it's best to fold them with tissue paper to cushion creases and store in a drawer.
6. Store sweaters on open shelves above separates for visibility. Make a stack of pullovers, cardigans, and turtlenecks. The best way to fold a sweater to keep it crease-free is to use the following steps:

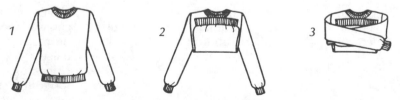

1

2

3

7. Don't hang fuzzy fabrics that shed like fur, suede, or mohair next to fabrics that attract lint like velvet, wool, corduroy.
8. Standard clip-style skirt hangers leave impressions in both real and synthetic suedes unless you protect the garment by tucking a scrap of medium to heavy weight fabric between waistband and clips.

Plan for Out-Of Season Storage

• Store clothes in dust-free, dry and cool areas to prevent mildew, and out of direct sunlight to prevent fading.

• A garment bag can hold hangers at the top and folded items at the bottom. Avoid plastic cleaners' bags for long term storage. They can be so airtight clothes can't breathe and mildew can develop.

• Create storage space with an extra rod installed above an existing one in a high ceiling closet, or behind the first rod in a deep one, or put a garment bag to the far side of your closet.

• Inexpensive portable clothes racks and underbed storage boxes can expand your available storage space. Or, use a pretty wicker chest or a foot locker. They can do double duty as tables.

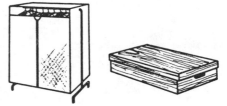

• Look for a dry-cleaner who will store clothing for you. There's usually a charge but it might be less than adding or building more storage space.

• Furs need professional reconditioning and cold storage during the off season to keep hairs strong and supple and to prevent skins from drying, cracking, and mildewing.

• Mothproofing is a must when the temperature is 50° or more. Air conditioning is no defense against moths! Scatter mothproofing crystals or balls liberally throughout all stored items using layers of tissue paper to prevent them from touching clothes. Do not use with leather or fur. Keep drawers and doors shut tightly or use garment bags and sealed boxes to confine the vapors as much as possible.

If you can't stand the smell of traditional mothproofing, look for lavendar scented varieties, or try our "Herbal Mothballs" recipe using ingredients available in health food or craft stores:

In your blender make a ground powder of equal parts of:

sassafras		thyme		cloves
lavendar	**or**	lavendar	**or**	caraway seeds
dried rue		woodruff		nutmeg
		rosemary		mace
				cinnamon
				tonquin beans

NOTE: Cedar chests, if airtight, keep out moths, but cedar does not kill moth larvae, the real culprit. Neither will herbal mixtures, but they do repel egg-laying moths because of their odor. If closets and clothes are clean and sealed as tightly as possible, they will do a good job keeping the enemy away.

Organize Your Fabric Stash

Do a closet cleanout just like you did with your clothes.
- Check for color first; if it's not "in your colors" or you no longer love it, discard.
- Tastes change. If you no longer love the appearance or hand of the fabric, discard.
- Evaluate printed fabrics carefully as they are easily outdated. Prints are related to the current trend in artistic style, so discard anything that isn't current.
- Consider the weight of the fabric. Heavy fabrics add visual pounds, so discard anything that is not flattering to you.

Dispose of your discards immediately before your emotions give you second thoughts.
- Give family and friends first choice.
- Have a fabric "swap meet". Measure and mark the yardage and fiber content and price; invite sewing friends and family to trade or buy.
- Include your unwanted pieces in a garage sale.
- Charitable organizations, schools, and rest homes are all grateful recipients of fabrics and that's worth a tax deduction for you.

Catalogue what's left so you'll have a workable reference.
- Use your "fabric on hand" catalogue as a guide for planning new sewing projects so you can blend what you have with new.
- Take your catalogue with you shopping, and on out-of-town trips when fabric shopping is a possibility.
- Here's how we catalogue our fabrics:
1. Buy a small telephone/address book with removable overlapping pages.
2. Cut a small swatch of fabric and attach it to the page.
3. Record additional information as illustrated below.
4. Organize pages in an order that makes sense to you:

by color	by weight (topweights,	by end use (blouse,
by fiber content	bottom weights)	skirt etc.)
by fabric type	by season	

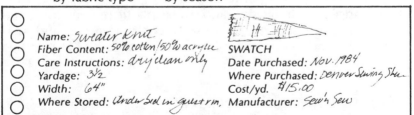

Name: *Sweater knit*
Fiber Content: *50% cotton/50% acrylic*
Care Instructions: *dry clean only*
Yardage: *3½*
Width: *64"*
Where Stored: *Under bed in guest rm.*

SWATCH
Date Purchased: *Nov. 1984*
Where Purchased: *Denver Sewing Shop*
Cost/yd. *$15.00*
Manufacturer: *Sew'n Sew*

Now use your system!
- Swatch and record each purchase **before** you put it away.
- When the sewing urge strikes, flip through your file.
- Take your catalogue to your closet to see what coordinates with your present wardrobe. Tack possible swatches to your bulletin board.
- Take your catalogue pages with you when shopping for coordinating fabric, linings, notions.

Store your fabric stash efficiently

1.   Preshrink fabrics before you put them away so they will be ready to sew when you are. Label them "preshrunk" to be sure.

2.   Mount inexpensive towel bars or a wooden ladder on the inside of a closet door. Carefully fold and drape fabrics over the "rods". Fabric is easy to see and dust-free!

3.   Commandeer a closet just for fabric storage. Remove the hanging rod and have shelves built from floor to ceiling. Organize fabrics by type — woolens on one shelf, cottons on another, or by use — bottomweights, topweights, or by color.

4.   Roll fabrics on cardboard tubes (ask for empties at your fabric store) and store in a pretty basket or in the closet. Some fabrics, especially very crisp ones and those with deep pile (crisp silk, linen, organdy, suede, velvet) are better rolled than folded to avoid sharp creases.

What to do with interfacings?

• If you have an **old** stockpile of unidentifiable fusible interfacings, toss or put them aside for craft projects. Replenish your stock with new.

• Get into the habit of buying your favorite interfacings in 3 to 5 yard lengths. You'll get better mileage out of the yardage and will always have a choice on hand.

• Roll fusible interfacings and their plastic instruction sheets onto cardboard tubes (paper towel rolls, gift wrap tubes) and tuck a label into one end. Store on a closet shelf, roll off what you need without creases.

What to do with fabric scraps??

• Store large scraps in boxes by fabric types (cotton, linen, silky, interfacing, etc.) and label them.

• Toss anything that isn't large enough to make something — a soft belt, a pretty scarf or neck bow.

What to do with your notions stash

• **Laces, tapes, trims (by the yard):** ask for an empty trim bolt at your fabric store and wrap your own trims. Wrap small yardages on index cards or small cardboard squares. Secure with a pin or a self adhesive label. You might want to swatch trims in your fabric reference catalogue.

• **Prepackaged tapes, trims, laces:** store in colorful plastic or metal file boxes well labeled with self adhesive stickers.

• **Thread:** baskets with lids (to keep the dust away) and clear plastic boxes with lids are great.

purchase a "threadbed" to hang close to the machine

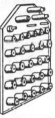

printers typecases are decorative storage

• **Buttons, zippers, hooks and eyes:** Organize by type and color in see-through plastic containers available in housewares and notions departments. Or buy metal hardware mini-chests with clear-front drawers. Swing Bins are also super.

If you are an antique buff, consider salvaging old pieces to put in your sewing room, for small storage and for large. An armoire outfitted with shelves and pull down table can become an entire sewing room. Barbara stores all her notions, sewing equipment, and even her sewing machine in a large Hoosier-style kitchen cabinet from the 1920's. It makes a great all in one sewing and storing center.

Make your pattern collection usable

1.   Keep a stock of favorite patterns — you can always create with your best design details. Marilyn Thelen, editor of **It's Me** magazine, calls these her "fashion reservoir". Remember that classic styles come and go, so it pays to buy a classic even though you may not plan to make it up immediately.

2.   Don't toss unwanted patterns, instead donate to family, friends, charitable organizations. (Save a few for the tissue for making alterations in new patterns.)

3.   Try one of these storage methods:
     • Leslie stores her patterns by style (tops, bottoms, jackets) in a small storage chest. She can pack them into a small space because she carefully puts them back into the envelope.

     • Store patterns you've used in 8½" × 11" manila envelopes or in file folders with the short ends taped shut. Cut pattern envelope open and mount with rubber cement on outside. File in file cabinet or cardboard file boxes available in office supply stores.

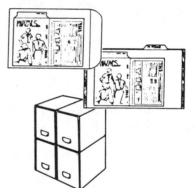

     • If file or drawer space is limited, store patterns in boxes and hide under a bed or in a closet. Fabric shops and mail order catalogues often offer cardboard pattern file boxes for standard size envelopes.

4.   Use your favorite patterns again and again:
     • Back the pattern tissue with fusible interfacing to prolong its life. Two products designed for this purpose are Pattern Saver (Pellon) and Back-A-Pattern (Stacy).

     • Sewing is easier the second time around if you do what Barbara does. She records the following:

On the pattern tissue
- *flat pattern measurements*
- *fitting adjustments made to pattern before cutting*
- *changes in fit or style made during construction.*

On the pattern envelope
- *date sewn*
- *weight and body measurements*
- *fabric used (attaches a swatch)*
- *interfacing used*
- *changes in sewing method*

Now it only requires a quick comparison to see if any changes would be needed the next time the same pattern is sewn.

Clothes Keeping

Our clothes are worth protecting for longer life and better looks. The following hints will help maximize the life of your investment.

1.   Air out clothes **on a hanger** overnight so wrinkles fall out and odors disappear. Dropping them in a pile results in more frequent cleaning and pressing which causes fading, shrinkage and loss of body.

2.   Take a cue from men who only clean their wool suits once or twice a year — brush clothes instead to get rid of fiber-breaking dust.

3.   Let your clothes rest between wearings so they have time to regain their shape.

4.   Remove pills with a "defuzzer" or whisk Dr. Scholl's callous remover gently over the surface of the fabric.

5.   Deodorant, perfume, and lotions all contain chemicals that damage fibers. Let them dry completely before dressing.

6.   Prevent snagging of hose by using a hand lotion before dressing.

7.   Stop runs with clear nail polish or Fray Check® (see page 95). To prolong the life of sandlefoot hose, paint the toe seam with Fray Check before wearing.

8.   Apply clear nail polish to rough edges on pins, chains, or pendants to keep them from snagging your clothes.

9.   Machine agitation turns small tears into gaping holes. Mend first.

Removing Stains

• Most spots can be removed completely with immediate attention. The longer a spot sits, the harder it is to remove.

• Never press over a spot. Heat will set the stain.

• Keep a good spot remover such as Goddard's Dry Clean on hand for quick attention to dry-clean only garments.

• Club soda is a favorite of flight attendants and waiters to prevent stains from setting.

• To remove a stain — put a clean, absorbent cloth under the fabric with the stain facing the cloth. Use a soft fabric to dab stain remover or water through the stain. Continue until stain is gone.

Perspiration — prevent the problem by wearing dress shields, especially with silks. With washables, pretreat fresh perspiration stains by flushing with a solution of ammonia and water. Rinse well.

Ink — water soluble hair spray dissolves ink on washable fabrics. Use rubbing alcohol on dry cleanables.

Oil — on silk, pretreat and wash with Easy Wash; on polyester, pre-treat with Spray 'N Wash, then wash.

Shall I Wash or Dry-Clean?

With ready-to-wear: Best to read and follow the care label instructions. We may think a fabric is washable (Ultrasuede® for example) but the manufacturer may have used a dry-clean only lining or interfacing.

With things you sew: You can be the one to determine washability. If you prewash your fabric, you can generally wash the finished garment. Read the fabric care information on the bolt end label, then pretreat by caring for the fabric as you will for the finished garment. Pretreat all accessory fabrics also. When you buy fabric remember to check the end of the bolt for care information. Copy it on to a card to file with a swatch of the fabric for future reference.

Care labels give you specific instructions on washing and drying. Generally, the finer the fabric the more likely it should be hand washed and air dried versus machine washed and dried.

Handwashing Silk

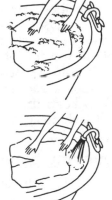

1. Draw lukewarm water (100°F) in bathroom sink for smaller pieces or the bathtub for larger pieces. Lukewarm water is best for removing soil and body oils. Add a mild liquid detergent like dishwashing types, or use a cold water detergent like Wool Tone by Van Wyck.

2. Swish garment for 1 - 2 minutes. Do not rub, squeeze, or twist — rubbing causes abrasion-related white spots, squeezing or twisting creates difficult wrinkles.

3. Rinse thoroughly in cold water (50°F). Cold water removes soap best and minimizes wrinkling.

4. Lay wet garment on a towel and roll up to blot out excess water.

5. Using a dry or steam iron at a low steam setting, iron garment until dry. If allowed to dry completely before ironing, wrinkles will be much harder to iron out, so only wash what you have time to press! (See **Sensational Silk** for complete information on the care and sewing of silk, ordering information on page 128.)

Handwashing Wool Sweaters

1.   Draw cool water. Add a cold water detergent like Wool Tone from Van Wyck (detergents work better in cool water than in cold).
2.   **Very gently** squeeze soapy water through sweater for 1 - 1½ minutes. Do not soak.
3.   Rinse twice in cold water.
4.   Pat out water, then roll in a towel to blot out more moisture.
5.   Dry sweater flat, blocking to original size if needed. (Tracing around sweater on Trace-A-Pattern® before washing will record original shape.)

Machine Washing Delicates

When the label recommends machine washing and drying, get the best results by following these tips:

1.   Turn garments wrong side out before washing to reduce abrasive wear on edges and creases.
2.   Use the slowest agitation speed and shortest wash cycle possible. Heat and agitation will wear out most clothes quickly, especially lingerie elastics.
3.   Use zippered mesh laundry bags, available in notions departments, for machine washing pantyhose and delicate blouses and lingerie. Use a **gentle** cycle.
4.   Over-drying is your clothes' worst enemy. It can cause static, pilling, progressive shrinkage, wrinkling, and puckered seams.
   -Use warm, not hot, heat to warm fabric and take wrinkles out.
   -Take clothes out of dryer while slightly damp and still warm. Shake well. Hang on a plastic hanger to cool and air dry.
   -Polyester thread in seams can shrink with excessive heat, causing puckered seams. If fabric is still slightly damp, you can tug gently on the seams to stretch the thread and eliminate puckers.

Dry-Cleaning — Get the Most for Your Money

1.   If an item in need of cleaning is part of a two-piece outfit, clean both pieces so they will remain the same color.
2.   Point out spots and stains to your cleaner and give the cause. Be sure to tell the cleaner the fiber content if you know it.
3.   Request that staples **not** be used to attach ID tags if you have no labels in your clothes, safety pins are much better.
4.   Remove delicate buttons or cover them tightly with aluminum foil before taking garments to the cleaners to avoid damage.
5.   Try "bulk dry-cleaning" for things like sweaters and items that don't require professional pressing. Generally, items in bulk cleaning are hung on hangers or folded with no pressing, but this service is really a money saver as it is priced by the pound.

6.   Overpressing is a real problem because it takes the life out of most fabrics. We've experienced many bad press jobs such as seam and hem edges showing through, creases where they don't belong, lapel roll lines in the wrong place. Ask your cleaner for a **soft** or a **light** press, or better yet, ask for "clean only" or "bulk dry-cleaning" at a much lower price. Many cleaners don't offer these services because of the extra care needed. They must hang everything as it comes out of the dry-cleaning machine so wrinkles don't set in. Normal procedure is to throw clothes in a heap and then professionally press later. We prefer to do our own touch-up pressing at home to solve the overpressing problem and save money at the same time! Be sure to see our tips on pressing that follow.

7.   Plastic cleaners' bags attract moisture and hold heat. Ask your dry cleaner not to bag your clothes until they are cool. Remove the bags before you put clean clothes into your closet so they can breathe.

8.   Keep your rainwear effective. Since water repellency decreases with wear, it should be renewed periodically. Treatment is available at most cleaners, and the additional charge is a good investment.

Pressing Matters

The right equipment for all your pressing needs, whether you're sewing or ironing after laundry, makes a big difference in the finished appearance and the ease of the task. You should have the following:

1.   **Good "shot-of-steam" type iron** with lots of holes in the bottom for fast pressing, a non-stick coating to help eliminate shine on fabrics, and a see-through water level gauge for timely refilling.

2.   **Well-padded ironing board.** We prefer cotton canvas ironing board covers; the metallic coated ones cause heat to bounce back and damage heat sensitive fabrics.

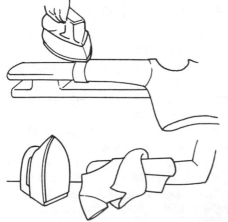

3.   **Sleeve board and pressing mitt.** These both make it easy to press sleeves (including full puff sleeves) without creases.

The pressing mitt will also allow you to tuck your hand inside a garment and safely reach difficult to press areas.

seam roll

press cloth

4. **Seam roll.** If you must press seams open again after cleaning, you can prevent unsightly seam edge impressions by tucking this under the seam while you press. This is often necessary in pants if you want flat slimming side seams.

5. **Cotton See-Through Press Cloths** (Dritz or June Tailor). Prevent shine, but allow you to see what you are doing.

6. **Hot Iron Cleaner** (Dritz Iron-Off or Stacy's Clean and Glide). A non-abrasive cleaner for keeping your soleplate clean and smooth. Use it on a hot iron with several layers of damp cloth.

7. **Iron sole plate covers** like Iron-All and Iron-Safe for pressing synthetics without creating shine. It is very important to remove them from your iron periodically to get rid of lint build-up and to prevent corrosion of the sole plate.

Some Pressing Hints

1. Always test iron heat on a scrap of fabric first to avoid the wrong temperature on your fabric — a too-hot iron can literally melt holes in synthetic fabrics.
2. Press delicate fabrics on the wrong side or use a press cloth or soleplate cover on the iron for top pressing.
3. Use a little spray starch or fabric finish (sizing) to keep lace, linen, and cotton crisp looking.
4. Fabrics have a memory only when cool. Be sure garments are cool before you move them or what you pressed in will fall out. Fabrics should be cool and dry before you put them back into the closet, and remember to allow a little breathing space between hanging items.
5. You can eliminate daily touch-up pressing by choosing the next day's clothing and placing them on a hook outside the closet so any closet wrinkles will hang out overnight.

Take Good Care of Shoes, Boots and Handbags...

... and you'll enjoy them for years! It starts when you buy. Since good shoes and handbags are so expensive, you may want to stick to pebble-textured or heavy calf skin for best wear.

• Give leather shoes and boots a paste polish before you wear them the first time. Future soil will penetrate less easily.

• Waterproof your footwear with a good silicone protector available in fine shoe repair shops. Read the instructions! The best formula is to spray, dry 4 or 5 hours, spray, dry, then polish.

• Patent leather and vinyl should be cleaned with a soft cloth dampened with white vinegar. Dry and shine with a soft cloth.

• Protect suede with a **stain repellent** spray. Use an artgum eraser or the Suede Stone cleaning bar (Tandy Leather Company) to remove minor soil. Rub stubborn spots with very fine sand paper. Restore the nap with a suede brush after removing surface dirt.

• If shoes or boots get wet, stuff them with crumpled tissue paper or newspaper and let them dry away from direct heat so they don't crack. Polish when thoroughly dry.

• Prevent rotting and stain damage from salt by wiping immediately with a half and half solution of white vinegar and water, or use a salt remover available in good shoe repair shops.

• Shoes and boots will last longer if you give them a day or more of rest between wearings to air out moisture and perspiration which can harden the inner shoe. Stuff shoes or boots with tissue, toe shapes or shoe trees to keep their shape and good looks longer.

• When better shoes show hard wear, they're worth repairing if the upper is still in good shape. Consider resoling and/or refinishing (redying and polishing). It's cheaper than buying new ones. We've had light colored shoes go through stages of tan to burgundy then to black.

• Handbags and briefcases should receive the same care treatment of water and stain resistant sprays, cleaning and polishing or brushing for longest life.

Travel in Style

We are part of an organization of 10 traveling professionals and packing lightly is a goal we all share. We feel that one suit and several blouses will get any professional woman through a business week on the road. The same philosophy can work for you for business or pleasure.

Remember The 5 Basic Pieces
add a few extra tops, one for evening

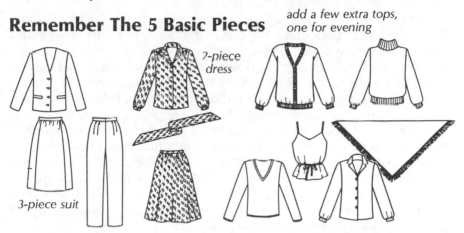

2-piece dress

3-piece suit

- Interchange skirt, pant, and blouses for versatility for the business or sightseeing day.
- A 2-piece dress gives you day and evening wear with a simple change of accessories.
- Pants can double as evening wear with a camisole and shawl or silky shirt and dressy belt.
- Pack a sweater for extra warmth to layer under your jacket or wear as a casual jacket look.
- Add a knit T-shirt or two (turtlenecks if the weather could be cool) to lend a casual air to the skirt or pant.

It's Important to Plan Ahead

1. Make a day by day list of what you'll be doing and what you need to wear for each activity. Plan outfits by the number of changes you need. (Leslie plans changes based on how often she wants to do hand wash in her hotel room.)
2. Consolidate where possible. You may not be seeing the same people every day, but if you do they will admire your know-how.
3. If you buy a new wardrobe for a trip, wear everything at least once so you'll know how to put the looks together and know they are comfortable to wear.

Plan Your Major Pieces First

1.   Use neutral colors for your main pieces so that everything goes with everything else. Darker neutrals and prints are best because they won't show soil or wrinkles as quickly.
2.   Pack easy-care fabrics. We love silk but prefer wash and drip-dry synthetics for travel. You can't beat knits for packability. Wool flannel, tweed, and gabardine travel well too, and Ultrasuede® brand fabric (a favorite!) is lightweight and wrinkle-free.
3.   Every top should go with every bottom. Tops are wardrobe extenders and weigh less than pants or skirts.
4.   Pack a lightweight black pant that can go from day to evening. Black is the best pant color for evening anywhere in the world, and can be teamed with tops of any color or style.
5.   Pack clothes that can do double duty like a blouse that can be worn as a jacket, or a shirtdress that can be a lightweight coat.
6.   Plan for weather extremes. Pack a lightweight blouse that could see you through an unexpected heat wave plus layers to add on in case the temperature drops. Turtleneck + shirt + sweater + raincoat can do it in just about any weather. Remember two pair of knee socks — one to wear and one to dry. (Socks are great slippers too).
7.   Choose your travel coat for the climate of your destination, but always plan for rain. A nylon cire raincoat can be rolled up into a corner of your tote bag. Because Ultrasuede® doesn't waterspot, it's perfect as a lightweight raincoat, too.

The Necessary Extras

1.   Accessories change the look of your basic pieces. Use color accents in scarves, belts, blouses to spice up your neutrals.
2.   Leave your valuable jewelry at home in the safety deposit box. If you must wear it, **DO NOT** pack it. Take only what you will wear and **wear it all the time**. Or check it in the hotel safe.
3.   Shoes are heavy so limit yourself to a comfortable day shoe and one pair for evening. For sightseeing, carry an extra pair in your tote bag. Don't let aching feet spoil your trip.
4.   If you must take boots, wearing them is easier than packing such a bulky item, but they can be uncomfortable on a long trip.
5.   Take a handbag that works with everything and pack a flat clutch for evening. Consider a lightweight tote bag for extra shoes, sweater, umbrella, camera, etc. for daily jaunts.
6.   Airplanes can be chilly, so tuck a sweater and socks into your carry-on bag along with a good book, needlework, hand sewing, or catch up on your paperwork like we do.

Proven Packing Tips from the Pros

About Suitcases:

1.   The size will make a big difference in how much your clothing will wrinkle. The larger 28" - 30" size allows you to lay jackets, skirts, and blouses flat with few, if any, folds. This means you have no carry-on luggage!

2.   A structured nylon hanging bag (the fold-over-to-carry type) is another choice. You can hang two or three blouses (or blouses with jackets) on one hanger that will also hold pants or skirts. Fold dresses over a hanger and pin at the waist. A shoulder strap is helpful for this lightweight, carry-on bag.

3.   We wouldn't travel without our "wheelies". Lightweight collapsible luggage carts and suitcases with built-in wheels save aching backs when porters are hard to find.

4.   Remove all previous baggage routing tags before you check your luggage, and double check your routing tags to make sure your bags have been sent to the right city! ALWAYS have name tags on both the outside **and** inside of your bags.

How To Pack

1.   Always pack the night before a trip and make a complete check-list. Take the list along in your purse or briefcase as an inventory in case your bags are lost. Do not pack valuables or medications; they go with you in your carry-on.

2.   Pack heavy items (travel iron, shoes) on the bottom of your suitcase at the hinged end. Noncrushables (lingerie, sweaters) go next, with easily wrinkled items on the top.

3.   Keep wrinkles to a minimum by packing each garment on its own hanger covered with a plastic cleaners' bag. Cleaners bags or tissue paper stuffed into sleeves also help to retain shape. Your own hangers make packing and unpacking go faster. Hotels do provide hangers, but often not enough, usually no skirt hangers, and those they do have are sized for men's clothing and not for women's!

4.   To pack pants, leave the legs hanging over the side of the suitcase while packing other clothes on top, then fold over on top when the suitcase is full. Do the same with dresses, packing skirt portion and allowing bodice to hang over the edge. Alternate the direction of necklines and bottom edges as you layer blouses and jackets.

5.   Pack your robe, nightgown and slippers on top so you can put them on first, then upack in comfort.

Keep Your Suitcase Organized — 14 Tips!

1.   Our favorite organizer is the clear (for easy visibility) zip lock plastic bag. The freezer weight, 10" × 12" size is the most versatile. Pack bras and panties in one, hose or scarves in another. Use smaller ones for cotton balls, vitamins, instant coffee (for those of you who carry an immersion heater). We carry extras for damp bathing suits, dirty laundry, etc. Such lifesavers! If plastic isn't your style, you can purchase coordinated lingerie and travel cases, or check the craft and accessory tabs at the back of the pattern catalogues for great accessories to sew.

2.   Pack shoes in their own cloth bags to keep them from soiling clothing. If color coded to the shoe color, it's easy to find the ones you need without opening all the bags! Leslie prefers one shoe to a bag — easier to tuck into a small empty space. Shoe bags are simple to make:

For each shoe bag: Stretch knit fabric 13" long × 10" wide
24" ribbon, shoelace, or cord for drawstring

1.   Turn down top edge ½" to form casing; stitch close to raw edge.

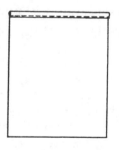

2.   Fold in half lengthwise, stitch ¼" seam across bottom and up side, leaving ¼" opening for casing. Backstitch to secure.

3.   Turn right side out. Insert ribbon, shoelace, or cord for drawstring.

3.   Keep shoes in shape by stuffing tissue paper tightly into the toes (or use sweet smelling toe sachets, see page 106) Or, save space by filling shoes with small items like lingerie, hosiery and belts.

4.   Pack silk flowers inside plastic containers like those used to package L'Eggs brand hosiery.

5.   Prevent damage to firm leather belts by placing them around the inner edge of the suitcase. Roll soft, crushable belts and tuck into corners.

6.   A plastic, portable salt shaker with snap-on lid is ideal for your bath powder. Use a 35mm film canister for face powder; it's just the right size for a make-up brush.

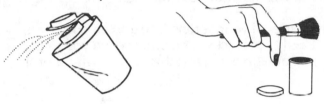

7.   Pack sample sizes of toiletries; they're ideal for travel and can be refilled from the at-home supply. Leakproof plastic containers are essential; squeeze bottles to remove air, then screw cap on tightly for an airtight seal that creates a vacuum and eliminates leaking. Pack nail polish and other liquid manicure essentials in separate, securely sealed zip lock bags to prevent disasters, and purchase nail polish remover in individual towelettes.

8.   Save perfume-scented papers that are sent as bill stuffers to tuck into your suitcase for sweet smelling clothes. (Keep them in stored luggage, too, to keep interiors fresh.) Don't forget to take your share of all the free perfume samples from the cosmetics departments. The tiny glass vials are perfect for travel; they contain several applications and don't take up any room in your cosmetics bag.

9.   A small roll of masking tape makes a great lint brush and more; use it to seal cosmetic bottle caps to prevent leaking, or as a temporary measure to hold up a loose hem.

10.   Carry a perfumed candle (the canned type with a lid is best) to scent your room. If stale smoke really bothers you, pack a can of spray air freshner or smoke dispelling spray (available in automotive stores and department store notions).

11.   If you travel with knits you'll want to include a Snag-Nab-It™ in your repair kit. Fray Check is another must to stop runs in hose and ravelling in fabric (see page 95). Goddard's Dry Clean or travel size spot remover is also a lifesaver. Look for individual foil packets at the drug store.

12. An empty prescription bottle or film canister makes a handy container for your travel sewing kit. Include thimble, hand sewing needles, a few straight pins tucked into a fabric scrap, small safety pins, and thread to match clothes you're packing wrapped onto a small piece of lightweight cardboard. Include a basic button or two, but the best button tip is to sew an extra one inside the front hem of each blouse you make. Small folding scissors are handy too.

13. Be sure to have a first aid kit with you. A small metal Band-Aids can that you fill with assorted items makes a great portable first aid kit.

14. Slip the barrel of your curling iron into an empty cardboard tube to protect it and to protect your clothes when you must pack it while it's still hot, or purchase a brand that comes with a protective cover for travel.

When You Arrive

1. Give your clothes a steam bath. Remove garments from plastic bags (store bags in your empty suitcase or the maid will throw them away!) and hang them on the shower curtain rod. Fill tub with hot, hot water and turn on the ceiling heat lamp (if available). Close the door securely. Within as little as 30 minutes to an hour, everything is pressed without an iron! Or, let the hot water run (be sure the drain is open!) to build up steam. Ten minutes with the door closed should do the trick. One important note: make sure the shower curtain rod is secure!

2. Call housekeeping to request an iron and ironing board, but don't count on their availability. Play it safe and carry a lightweight portable iron or clothes steamer, and turn the covers back on the bed for a smooth padded ironing surface. Or place a fluffy towel on the table as an ironing board; the floor works too. Don't forget to tuck a press cloth in the corner of your suitcase for top pressing on delicate fabrics. When space permits, we pack the "tailors sleeve pad" from June Tailor (available in fabric stores). It's particularly helpful in pressing sleeves without forming a crease down the center. The June Tailor "cushioned pressing pad" is another small (16" × 12") piece you might want to pack. It's a vast improvement over pressing on the bed.

If You're A Frequent Traveler

It is worth the investment to keep an extra set of travel items packed in your luggage so packing is easier and faster. Tailor the following list to suit your needs:

1. Cosmetics, toiletries, and a hairbrush in a cosmetic bag
2. Manicure set (include foil wrapped polish remover)
3. Shower cap and disposable razors (we've left good ones behind too many times!)
4. Curling iron, hot curlers, blow-dryer, and mirror in compact travel sizes
5. Small travel iron or clothes steamer
6. Extension cord (hotel outlets are never where you need them)
7. Heating pad (perfect for aches, pains, and cold rooms)
8. Foil wrapped spot remover
9. Nightgown, robe and slippers
10. Swimsuit, leotard and tights (just in case the urge to exercise does hit. Hotels often have free workout rooms, saunas, pools)
11. Jogging clothes for the same reasons above
12. Travel alarm clock
13. Small fold up umbrella, sunglasses
14. Swiss army knife
15. Coffee kit (cup, spoon, immersion heater, instant coffee, powdered "cream", dehydrated soups, instant oatmeal)
16. Small scissors, small stapler and staples, tape
17. Writing kit (stationery, envelopes, extra stamps)
18. Small notebook for purse or briefcase to record expenses, contacts, interesting places, restaurants
19. Tape recorder (great for dictating notes while driving. Make your own favorite music or exercise tapes.)
20. Earplugs (just in case you don't like listening to your neighbor's snoring, or if you are in an airport hotel)
21. Portable smoke alarm; small flashlight
22. Small camera
23. Sleep mask

Index

Bibliography

The following is a list of publications we feel have special information that would be valuable for you to read:

The Complete Bonnie August Dress Thin System by Bonnie August, Rawson, Wade Publishers, New York.

Conservative Chic by Amelia Fatt, Times Books, New York.

The Fashion Survival Manual by Judie H. McQuown and Odile Laugier, Everest House Publishers, New York.

Hot Tips, 1000 Fashion and Beauty Tricks by Frances Patiky Stein, G.P. Putnam's Sons, New York.

Looking Terrific by Emily Cho and Linda Grover, G.P. Putnam's Sons, New York.

Sew Big — A fashion guide for the fuller figure, by Marilyn Thelen, Palmer/Pletsch Associates, Portland, OR.

Short Chic by Allison Kyle Leopold and Ann Marie Cloutiers, Rawson, Wade, New York.

Taking Care of Clothes by Mablen Jones, St. Martin's Press, New York.

"W", a weekly newspaper published by Fairchild Publications (write Subscription Service, PO Box 2601, Boulder, CO 80321)

More Products from Palmer/Pletsch!

Palmer/Pletsch publishes a whole series of easy to use, information-filled sewing how-to books. Look for their books and new video in local fabric stores or order through Palmer/Pletsch by copying the form below.

new!

Original ROO
A children's story that makes sewing fun!